dixi
books

# Mark Tedesco

Mark Tedesco is a writer and educator residing in California. Having lived in Italy for eight years, he enjoys weaving stories connecting the present to the longings are expressed in relationships, events, culture, and history.

Mark has written in the genres of travel, historical fiction, memoir, self-help and children's fiction. His titles include: *That Undeniable Longing, I am John I am Paul, Lessons and Beliefs, The Dog on the Acropolis and Loving Hoping Believing.* Mark's Dixi Books title, *She Seduced Me: A Love Affair with Rome,* brings to life Mark's love for the magic of a city, in which he weaves history, personal stories and interviews into a tale that, little by little, also seduces the reader.

Besides writing, Mark is an educator, and he loves to engage his students in his love of history, literature and each person's unique story. In his off time, Mark likes to travel, but, somehow, he always ends up returning to Rome where, he is convinced, other stories are waiting to be uncovered.

# She Seduced Me

## A Love Affair with Rome

### Mark Tedesco

**Dixi Books**

Copyright © 2020 by Mark Tedesco
Copyright © 2020 Dixi Books

She Seduced Me: A Love Affair with Rome - Mark Tedesco
Editor: Katherine Boyle
Proofreading: Andrea Bailey
Designer: Pablo Ulyanov
I. Edition:  November 2020

Library of Congress Cataloging-in Publication Data
Mark Tedesco
ISBN: 978-1-913680-04-6
1. Travel writing  2. Italian life 3.  Ancient Roman history 4. Travel tips

© Dixi Books Publishing
293 Green Lanes, Palmers Green, London, England, N13 4XS

info@dixibooks.com
www.dixibooks.com

# She Seduced Me

## A Love Affair with Rome

**Mark Tedesco**

dixi
books

*The Voice of the New Age*

# Chapters

# Introduction

I resisted, but she drew me back. I stayed away, but she beckoned me. I distanced myself, but she haunted me. I even rejected her, but she did not abandon me.

What is it about Rome that seduces the heart, fascinates the mind, and envelops the senses? Once she becomes part of you, there is no turning back, no forgetting, no forsaking. Her fascination deepens with the passing of time and the maturity of life. I cannot stay away for more than a year, and even that is not enough. She is like a jealous lover, a siren, or a genie who casts an enchanting spell from which one does not want to escape.

I was nineteen when I first visited Rome, and, though knowing only bits and pieces of ancient history, I found myself drawn in by the monuments, the energy, and the magic of the place. If I had to come up with one word to describe Rome, it would be "magical." Churches with miraculous stories, empty roads at night in the Roman Forum filled with the whispers of the spirits of Patricians, slaves and plebeians making their way towards the temples, street performers for thousands of years making visitors laugh, smiling tourists and pilgrims who would not want to be anywhere else, sinners, saints, and weirdos all taking the same strolls down the same roads at the same time. Magnificent. Magical. Fascinating.

But what could a teenager understand about the glories of Rome? I was in the seminary, and our father superior was Padre Bonuccelli, which translates as Father Goodbirds. Our dwelling was outside of Rome near Tivoli. Every school day, forty seminarians and I drove into Rome in our minivans to the Angelicum, where we listened to lectures on historical philosophy, ontology, and the social sciences. Father Goodbirds continually warned us about Pagan Rome (Roma Pagana) and the dangers of exploring the city, but eventually, my curiosity got the better of me. After a few months of attending the Italian lectures, I ditched class, whipped out my map, and headed towards San Pietro in Vincoli, just a twenty-minute walk from the university.

Walking into the church and heading straight towards the massive statue of Moses by Michelangelo, I stopped in awe, fixed in my place, and looked up. I recalled the story of the artist who, upon completion of the Moses, threw his hammer at the sculpture and shouted, "Speak!!!" I whispered under my breath: "Speak…" I don't know how many minutes passed before I became aware of time again; glancing at my watch, I turned to rush back to the university before I would be missed. But before leaving the church I felt that I now carried something within me which wasn't there when I entered. I brought a spark of magic with me.

That day was a new beginning: Rome would be mine, I would be hers, and no one could take that away.

# Chapter 1
## Stories, Saints, and Weirdos

One's first impression of Rome is often colored by the number of priests and nuns everywhere. In the gelaterias, taking walks, getting on busses, chatting with friends, shopping for underwear (yes, I've seen this), eating at restaurants, riding bicycles, and ordering cappuccinos. They act like they own the place! And yet, in a way, they do.

By the time the Visigoths sacked Rome in 410 CE, Rome had fallen into such decline that the citizens were starving. The population of the city dropped from a million to a low point of 17,000; Rome was almost abandoned, and when the Visigoths arrived, they were welcomed by the remaining Romans in the hope that they would bring them something to eat. The Goths plundered the city, moved on, and Rome became a ghost town. Buildings were dismantled, artifacts carried away, and the coliseum was used as a landfill. The once-great empire was shattered, the unifying Roman government was gone, and the military was in shambles. The greatness of Rome was no more.

IIn 1447, upon becoming Pope, Nicholas V brought with him a vision of what Rome could be. Monuments, fountains, wide boulevards, libraries, and art collections were ideas that inflamed the Renaissance Pope's imagination. Today, while gazing on the Trevi Fountain, for example, Nicholas's hand can be seen. The waters of the Aqua Virgo, feeding the font, had been cut off and diverted to other areas. Still, Nicholas envisioned the restoration of the fountain as a celebration of the waters feeding the city. Though the present sculptural group is the product of a long evolution of fountain designs, it was the vision of the first Renaissance Pope, Nicholas V, that brought us a celebration in stone where there was only a dried up aqueduct.

Nicholas was a Renaissance bookworm. His passion led him to lay the foundations for the Vatican Library, for which he employed scholars and humanists to gather and copy ancient and contemporary texts. His vision was to establish Rome as a destination for scholars, and Nicholas saved many Greek works that otherwise would have been lost. His humanistic vision extended beyond theology to all areas of knowledge.

Nicholas V's dreams were bigger than his capacity to realize them, and it would take subsequent Popes, such as Sixtus IV (after whom the Sistine Chapel is named) and Julius II, to bring these dreams to fruition. Under Sixtus, Rome was transformed from a Medieval to a Renaissance city, accomplishing such works as the construction of the Sistine Chapel, founding the Vatican Archives, and expanding the Vatican Library. But it was Julius II (reigning from 1503 to 1513), with his impulsive and aggrandizing character, who transformed Rome into a world center of architecture, art, culture, and learning. Looking up at the ceiling of the Sistine Chapel, one can almost hear Pope and artists, Julius and Michelangelo, struggling to make their visions a reality, even though Michelangelo insisted that he was no painter while creating the frescoed ceiling. Julius also initiated the new St. Peter's Basilica, and employed Raphael to produce his magnificent frescoes in Vatican City, including his *School of Athens*. The Pope went on to hire Bramante to unite the Vatican with the Belvedere, conceived the Court of St. Damasus with its loggias, and the Via Giulia with its beautiful buildings and commissioned Michelangelo's colossal statue of Moses, from which this story takes its starting point.

This brief overview of papal sponsorship of the arts in Rome isn't exhaustive nor aims to gloss over the disastrous personal lives, political ambitions, or questionable faith of the persons involved. But with all that Papal sponsorship, I ask myself, what right do I have to object to all the priests and nuns infiltrating every nook and cranny of Roman life?

So let's get back to Rome's history as we explore two aspects: buildings and their stories, and the people who live in and flock to the Eternal City.

"There was an earthquake at the moment of the crucifixion; it produced this crack in the rock, so a chapel was built to commemorate this event," was the story shared with me when I was touring Italy as a seminarian in the 1980s. "This painting was made by St. Luke and was found in a river by a shepherd; he brought it to the bishop. That is why there is a church built on this spot," was another story. "The angels carried this house from Ephesus to Loreto; this is the house where the Virgin Mary lived," was another one. Fifteen of us, mostly Americans, were touring Italy under our Italian priest's guidance, who wanted to expose us to his country's faith experience. After visiting several shrines constructed to commemorate the Virgin Mary's appearances, I couldn't keep silent anymore. "The Virgin Mary must not like heaven very much," I blurted out. All faces in the van turned towards me. "Why?" asked a pious Italian fellow seminarian. "Because she's always in Italy!" I said. Americans chuckled, Italians fumed.

But after becoming more immersed in Italian culture, I realized that it is the story that matters. There is barely a building, a monument, or a crevice that does not have an anecdote attached to it, and the story is what gives meaning. At first, this was difficult for me, coming from a scientific black and white outlook, but my appreciation for the storytelling in Italy grew.

I knew little of the Church of St. Paul at the Three Fountains in Rome, except that it was the site where the apostle was supposedly martyred. Off the tourist maps, I was intrigued to go there and discover the site for myself. Since there are many churches in that area, I located a sign that indicated the one designated as the "Place of Martyrdom of Saint Paul the Apostle, where three springs miraculously gushed out." Water gushing? I didn't see any, so I went inside and found a pillar where the sign indicated, St. Paul was bound. Picking up a pamphlet, I read that there had been three fountains on this spot, which were currently tapped off due to pollution. These three fountains mark the three places where St. Paul's head bounced three times when he was beheaded, water springing up miraculously. Did it really happen? Does it matter? It is the story that is important.

Not only Christian Rome has its stories.

A stone is just a stone, but not in Rome. Walking through the Forum, there is a sizeable covered rock just off the Via Sacra where, inevitably, one will find flowers laid on that stone, day after day, year after year, century after century. To the unsuspecting tourist, this is just another mound cluttering the once glorious Forum. But the story of that stone reaches back to the time of Julius Caesar, hated by some, revered by others and respected by all. On the Ides of March, Caesar walked into the place where the Senate was meeting where he was stabbed 23 times by his enemies, and those he believed were his friends. The city fell into shock and disintegrated into warring factions, but there had to be a funeral and a reading of his last testament. Mark Anthony obtained Caesar's will from the house of the Vestal Virgins and brought it to that rock, the funeral pyre where Ceasar's body was to be cremated. The entire city gathered in front of that spot and brought pieces of furniture, wood scraps, logs, and fuel so that the pyre was several stories tall. As the flames engulfed the body and the flickering light illuminated the onlookers' faces, Mark Anthony eulogized Caesar while many in the crowd wept.

## Antony

*Friends, Romans, countrymen, lend me your ears;*
*I come to bury Caesar, not to praise him.*
*The evil that men do lives after them;*
*The good is oft interred with their bones;*
*So let it be with Caesar. The noble Brutus*
*Hath told you Caesar was ambitious:*
*If it were so, it was a grievous fault,*
*And grievously hath Caesar answer'd it.*
*Here, under leave of Brutus and the rest--*
*For Brutus is an honourable man;*
*So are they all, all honourable men--*
*Come I to speak in Caesar's funeral.*
*He was my friend, faithful and just to me:*
*But Brutus says he was ambitious;*
*And Brutus is an honourable man.*
*He hath brought many captives home to Rome*
*Whose ransoms did the general coffers fill:*
*Did this in Caesar seem ambitious?*
*When that the poor have cried, Caesar hath wept:*
*Ambition should be made of sterner stuff:*
*Yet Brutus says he was ambitious;*
*And Brutus is an honourable man.*
*You all did see that on the Lupercal*
*I thrice presented him a kingly crown,*
*Which he did thrice refuse: was this ambition?*
*Yet Brutus says he was ambitious;*
*And, sure, he is an honourable man.*
*I speak not to disprove what Brutus spoke,*
*But here I am to speak what I do know.*
*You all did love him once, not without cause:*
*What cause withholds you then, to mourn for him?*
*O judgment! thou art fled to brutish beasts,*
*And men have lost their reason. Bear with me;*

*My heart is in the coffin there with Caesar,*
*And I must pause till it come back to me.*

(Shakespeare, Julius Caesar, Act III Scene 2).[1]

When the crowds dispersed, the fire became embers, and Caesar's bones were gathered up; the rock remained where all this had taken place, that same rock where flowers are laid today.

What do a church and noisy crows have in common? Heading over to the glorious Piazza del Popolo, standing in the middle facing north, there is a church, Santa Maria del Popolo, which marks the spot where a large walnut tree once grew. I tried to imagine the tree in place of the church 1,000 years ago, and the people, residents, and visitors avoiding that area because the crows perched on its branches would swoop down and attack. Not one crow, but a whole flock lived in that walnut tree and fought against human encroachment. Why were these evil crows always up for a fight?

The story had been handed down that Nero, one of the most hated Roman emperors, had been buried in this area. Could the noisy crows and Nero's burial place be connected?

"His body lies under the tree; a landslide covered his tomb," residents whispered. "The crows embody his demonic spirit," visitors swore. "The roots draw up his evil influence and deposit it in any living thing passing by," others warned. As the stories grew, so did the fear; some began to avoid the Porta Flaminia because of these stories. Someone had to do something about this evil influence; the Church had to do something.

In 1099, the populace finally convinced the Pope, Paschal II, to organize a procession down the Via Flaminia, with a crucifix leading the people and an ax in the Pope's hand; Paschal was determined to put an end to Nero's influence forever. Reaching that spot, the Pope took the ax, struck low and hard at the trunk,

---

1 William Shakespeare, The Tragedy of Julius Caesar, comp. Barbara A. Mowat and Paul Werstine (New York: Washington Square Press, 2005).

until the tree fell, and the crows flew off in a panic. The legend continues that Nero's remains were found intertwined in the roots; his bones were removed and thrown into the Tiber. Then, to commemorate the triumph of good over evil, a makeshift church was built on this spot, from which this present church takes its origin.

A huge walnut tree, angry crows, a Roman emperor, and a baroque church; what could these possibly have in common?

Another story begins with Christmas in Bethlehem, continues with bad Roman weather in August, and goes on to the Spanish discovery of the Americas, which results in the church known as St. Mary Major. Less touristy than the Vatican, it has a more devotional atmosphere inside, whereas outside, it looks like a cold stone structure in the middle of a parking lot. The decor is typically baroque without anything unique or exciting until one hears the stories.

The history began in Bethlehem when Christ was born about 4 BCE in a stable because there was no room at the inn (Luke 2:7). Sources say that the baby was laid in a manger, which becomes the focus of our story. The manger is a type of open trough for animals to feed from, consisting of legs or a stand and the trough itself, made from wood or stone. Helena, the mother of Constantine, traveled to the Middle East to secure the places sacred to Christians, including the place of Christ's birth, converting the cave into a chapel and then into a basilica. The history here becomes vaguer, but a reference to Christ's crib appearing in Rome surfaces under the pontificate of Pope Theodore (640-649). Under the high altar of St. Mary Major's can be seen a glass bubble with five wooden boards visible that are said to be part of the manger carried to Rome from Bethlehem at the time of Pope Theodore.

The next phase of the story is a summer snowstorm; it was August 5, 352 CE, when snow purportedly fell on the Esquiline Hill in Rome. Before the snow could melt, the people marked the outline; the snow was interpreted as a sign that a church should be built on that spot in honor of the Virgin Mary. The present basilica dates back to the fifth century CE with additions and renovations through the centuries. The third part of our story begins with the Spanish colonization of the Americas.

In 1532, the Spaniards made contact with the mighty Inca empire, and in about twenty years, Pizarro and the Spanish conquistadors had conquered the Incas and took possession of their wealth. Peru then became an essential Spanish colony, providing gold and silver for another 300 years. Pizarro and his brothers destroyed the Inca empire. These original conquistadors became extraordinarily wealthy. From these events, the myth of El Dorado was born, which referred to a lost land filled with riches that waited to be discovered. This myth inspired Europeans, especially the poor and uneducated, to move to South America in search of wealth. The consequences of these events were tragic but also gave rise to the Latin American people and culture.

Amid the destruction of the Inca empire, our story finds its place. Sitting inside St. Mary Major, looking up at the coffered ceiling, the gold in that ceiling is said to have been brought back to Spain from the Inca invasion and donated to the Church by Isabell and Ferdinand of Spain.

Snow in August, invasions in South America, and a voyage to Bethlehem are some of the stories that are as important to the structure of this church as are its stones, mortar, and glass of which it is made.

I analyzed, scoffed at, criticized, or attempted to reinterpret these stories to suit my taste in the past. But then I realized that it doesn't matter if they are fact, legend or fantasy for the Romans who are surrounded by these stories. They don't get hung up on this. The stories are like an oral history, which gives meaning to the black and whiteness of life.

The soul of Rome lies not only in its buildings and stories but especially in its people. As we explore the city's religiosity, the people in Rome fall mostly into four categories: saints, sinners, weirdos, and the indifferent.

While a student in Rome, I decided to volunteer at a homeless shelter run by Mother Theresa's nuns at St. Gregorio, behind the coliseum. Once a week, after my studies, I would make my way to the shelter and help out with dinner, chat with the men, and support the sisters any way I could. The nuns started this shelter a few years previous, utilizing an available residence next to the large church. The word was that the sisters slept in a converted chicken coop in back.

The sisters seemed bright and cheerful, and the residents seemed grateful. One evening I was asked to do an intake. "He has been living on the streets and has to be bathed and given new clothes. We burn their old clothes, so leave them in the bathroom. These men are scared of water, so they will need two of you to help bathe him," the sister said to me and my companion. I had never bathed someone before, but I reluctantly agreed. My companion Robert had done this type of work and was more confident.

We ran the water in the tub, put some soap in, and this homeless man we will call Stefano entered. "We are going to help you get cleaned up; go ahead and remove your clothes," Robert said. Stefano hesitated, so we turned away as he removed his clothing. "Go ahead and get into the tub," Robert encouraged him. When I turned to bag his used clothing, I noticed that he had been defecating in his pants for some time; I left them where they were on the chair.

"Here is a sponge; go ahead and wash, and we can help wash your back," Robert encouraged Stefano. Within two or three minutes, the water in the bathtub was jet black. "We will drain this and draw another bath," Robert continued.

I had let Robert take the lead; at a certain point, between the black water and the odor, I felt nauseous and dizzy. "Be back in a minute," I said to Robert, as I stepped out the door. Some minutes later, I stepped back in, and Robert was finishing up the second bath. He was good-spirited, whereas I was extra baggage. Once Stefano got out of the tub, I stepped forward to do something useful. "Let me clean the tub," I said and began scrubbing it with a brush and running water. "Let's do it together," Robert added, and we both bent down to sanitize the tub for the next bather. Once finished, we turned around and discovered that Stefano had put on his old crap filled clothes again. Robert and I looked at each other, sighing. "Take those off and put on these new clothes," he said. He then turned to me and added, "Let's just wipe him down rather than doing another bath," and I nodded.

Once finished for that evening, we took the bus back to the seminary and I got in the shower and stood there for about thirty minutes, scrubbing intensely. Once clean, I felt good that I had accomplished another week of volunteer work for the homeless and now could return to my routine.

Later that evening in my room, I thought of Mother Theresa's sisters at San Gregorio's. They did this work all day every day, not only a few hours a week like I did; they did not distance themselves from the homeless like I did; they were not disgusted by the smells and sights like I was. They didn't seek attention or acclaim for their work; they seemed happy and joyful, as they joked with residents and volunteers. What was it that gave them this spark?

When I think of the saints in Rome, I think of Mother Theresa's sisters at San Gregorio.

Another phenomenon found in Rome more than anywhere else is the presence of communities and movements which focus on living the charism or particular aspect of faith that brings it alive for its members. Stumbling into Santa Maria in Trastevere just about any evening of the week at 8:30 p.m., one encounters the community of Sant' Egidio, chanting psalms and reflecting on the implications of a faith experience.

What I find fascinating about the community of Sant' Egidio is its spontaneous origins and universal outlook. It started when a group of young people decided to meet together to pray the psalms and to understand the implications of their faith. These beginnings led the community to support refugees fleeing violence, feed the homeless, find work for immigrants, support addicts on their way to recovery, nurse the terminally ill, work for a solution to the AIDS crisis and even negotiate peace between countries and peoples (Albania, Mozambique, Algeria, Congo, and others). Yet its message is simple: the basis of their communal life is their evening prayer, and their social work can be summed up as "friendship with the poor."

It is the simplicity and effectiveness of St. Egidio's community life that struck me because it is not based on an ideology.

One evening, after attending their evening prayer service in Trastevere and listening to the community pray for the all-but-forgotten Syrian refugees, I found myself saying to my friend Jerry: "This is what Christianity is supposed to be!"

But Rome has its share of sinners, as I realized one day when I brought a pair of my shoes to a cobbler's shop near the Vatican. "Pig God!" he shouted as he struck his thumb rather than the sole of the shoe he was pounding. "Pig Virgin!" he cried out again, blaming the residents of heaven for his lousy aim. Blasphemy. It is a language little used in the English speaking world, in which a sacred name is coupled with the lowest life form that the speaker can imagine. It was odd to gaze at this unhappy man, working day after day in his cobbler shop, crying out to blame others and filling the space with anger. I resolved not to return.

Scamming is another pastime in Rome that is not in the sacred realm. Whether it be pickpocketing a tourist, shortchanging a foreigner, overcharging an American, or the perpetually broken credit card machine ("Mi dispiace, non funziona; solo cash[2]"). Whether it falls into the category of "sin" is another debate, but some Romans feel justified in taking advantage of naive foreigners to make ends meet. For decades the 64 bus line, from the train station to the Vatican, has been notorious for pickpockets and thieves. It is also known for the too-close-for-comfort stance that some men take when the bus is crowded. But if caught in the act,

---

2 "I am sorry, the credit card machine doesn't work; only cash."

the perpetrator will inevitably be outraged that one could accuse him of such a thing. Best to keep all belongings in one pocket or bag, keep one's hand or arm snuggly over it, and avoid the situation altogether. Or, better yet, walk.

Shortchanging, overcharging, and the broken credit card machine are all symptoms of the same mentality: the system is rigged against the shop owners who have to find ways to get on equal footing. Visiting Rome means the foreigner has enough money to part with to help the owners make a living and support a family under an oppressive bureaucratic system, making it challenging to run a business in Rome. The end justifies the means, and if the visitors return home with a few dollars less because he/she was shortchanged, nobody got hurt. After all, rules are for humans, not humans for rules, right?

But what about sex in Rome? Sexual norms in the city are not as black and white as in the United States or the United Kingdom. Sometimes the lines between hetero and homosexual orientation are blurred; fidelity in marriage is an ideal that one aims at but doesn't attain, and church moral teachings are praised but not practiced. All of this is exemplified in the notorious 64 bus, known not only for pickpocketing but also for sex.

For decades this specific bus has been known as the place where one could lose not only one's wallet but also one's virginity. Foreigners who live in Rome see this, if not by experience, then by witnessing it play out.

I was on the crowded 64, trying to make it across town to make a meeting near the Vatican when the bus took a sharp turn, and we all grabbed tight as the bus shifted, and we struggled to maintain our places. The man in front of me changed stance as we took the turn and backed into me; rather than taking his original place, he remained pressed against me. Since I had another person right behind me, I could not shift positions. Frozen in place, I wondered what was happening; as his body pressed more tightly against mine, it soon became apparent. At the next bus stop, I squeezed through the crowd and hopped off. Afterward, I wondered how it would have played out if I had stayed on that bus.

Another time on this same bus line, I was standing towards the back and had a clear view of the crowded bus center. An elderly well-dressed Italian woman sat in the aisle seat, looking out the window. Next to her was a scraggly looking Italian man, perhaps in his forties, carrying a small briefcase. I noticed that he held the briefcase above the older woman's leg and slowly lowered it. Fascinated, I watched the scene, moving positions to get a more unobstructed view. He briefly touched her leg with the suitcase, then lifted it. The woman kept looking out the window, perhaps assuming that someone had jostled the passengers. The man lowered the briefcase onto her leg once more, this time keeping it there. After a few seconds, what was happening seemed to dawn on the woman, who shifted her leg, looked up in annoyance and fear, and scooted further away from her love interest. Discovered and exposed, the man slinked to the back of the bus.

Everyone who lives in Rome and takes the 64 bus line regularly has similar stories. Is such flirting dangerous? Not in my experience. But one may find that not only has he/she left his wallet on that bus but also one's innocence.

We have covered saints and sinners in Rome, but we cannot forget the most prolific group: the weirdos.

You see them in the churches, you see them on the streets and in the piazzas. There is the barefoot Franciscan who believes he is the reincarnation of St. Francis of Assisi. A priest dressed in a spotless black cassock with a collar so high that he cannot nod. A man who stays in churches all day and goes from Mass to Mass, consuming communion as if he did not need other nourishment. Laypeople and clergy who believe they see divine visions and are destined to do great things as they strive to gather followers. Every type of person whose religiosity and humanity are either out of sync or whose religiosity has completely suppressed their humanity seems to end up in this city.

I lived with one of these weirdos during my first year in the seminary in Rome, a certain Brother Gino, who was later ordained as a priest. He claimed to have visions of the Virgin Mary, bore the wounds of Christ (the stigmata), and that God used him to communicate with pilgrims. We, seminarians, lived with him at a shrine outside of Rome, and hundreds of people came every week to pray in the sanctuary and see "il santo." Gino founded an order of nuns and believed he was called to bring renewal to the whole Church. It all sounded good to me, nineteen years old at the time, as I began my studies in Rome. Could this be an extraordinary man of God, who smelled like flowers whenever he walked by, a scent his followers called the "odor of sanctity"?

I seemed invisible to this Gino until he invited me to his private meeting room, where he spent time with visitors who requested his counsel. He looked at me with his big black eyes and asked me to sit next to him. I opened up to him about my struggles at home and in the seminary, and he encouraged me to move forward without fear. "If God hadn't meant you to be here, He would have put obstacles in your way to prevent you from coming," was his advice. Then he rose from his chair and opened his arms to embrace me. I accepted the embrace of "il santo" as he kissed my cheek. He then pushed me out a little and made the sign of the cross on my chest. "This heart belongs to me," he said. He then tugged at my shirt to lift it and pressed my bare chest against him. I felt confused and became aroused, having been embraced so few times in my life; I stood still and stiff as a board, hoping the saint would not perceive my arousal. After a while, seeing no overtures on my part, he concluded our encounter, asked me to tuck in my shirt, and thanked me for coming. During the months after this encounter, he (and I) behaved as if nothing had happened, and I became invisible to Gino again.

At nineteen, I didn't know how to interpret this episode but, years later, when Gino got suspended by the Vatican for molesting seminarians, it all made sense.

Stories, monuments, saints, sinners, and weirdos all make up the beautiful complexity of Rome.

# Chapter 2
# Life in the Streets

In 462 BCE, Roman law (*The Law of the Twelve Tables*) first mentions street performers, making it a crime to parody the government or its representatives in public places. Though this law was not always enforced, its presence signals a flourishing culture of street entertainment not only in Rome but also in the ancient world. Given that this law attempted to control  government leaders' criticism, we can deduce that street entertainment in ancient Rome often had political connotations.

Street performances in ancient Rome included simple plays, acrobatics, and perhaps even puppetry. Through this entertainment, the people had a voice, and the performers were able to earn non-taxed income.

Romans spent much of their free time in the streets, evidenced by the many food stalls, public temples, and speaking platforms, such as the Rostra in the Forum. Living inside small multilevel apartments without kitchens or baths, the lower classes flocked to the baths, the stadiums, and the streets for political commentary, nourishment and entertainment.

But where would street performers be found in ancient Rome? They were probably everywhere Romans would assemble, and no other venue drew a more diverse daily crowd than the baths; the most massive bath structures were that of Diocletian and Caracalla. Much of Diocletian's baths' remaining structure was converted into a church, a monastery, and subsequently into a museum. To get the "vibe" of a day at a Roman bath, and the entertainment offered, one has to head to Thermae Caracalla, the Baths of Caracalla.

Any bust of Emperor Caracalla depicts him as a handsome man with an expression halfway between being constipated and pissed off. The emperor saw himself as bigger than life and aspired to be a sort of reincarnation of Alexander the Great. Still, he could never get past his ego, cruelty, and insatiable hunger for glory and admiration. Having his brother Geta killed to eliminate any competition for the throne, he went on to kill his brother's friends and associates. Caracalla also got rid of his wife, first exiling her and then having her killed too.

Caracalla's father Lucius Septimus Severus began the construction of the baths and named him after his son, who knew that grande public works could win the people over. According to the historian Herodian[3], Caracalla was in constant conflict with his brother and, even as a child, was mean-tempered and spent much of his youth engaged with cockfighting, chariot racing, dancing, and going to shows. He was, in other words, a playboy who combined the unlikable qualities of a total lack of responsibility with unbridled jealousy and ambition. Perhaps Severus understood what type of man his son was becoming and that he would need to construct something truly breathtaking, with Caracalla's name all over it, for the people to be won over. Hence the Baths of Caracalla were initiated in the year 206 BCE, when Severus was still alive, and completed around the year 216 BCE once Caracalla was in power.

Apart from tourists, today, the Baths are in a tranquil setting by Roman standards, surrounded by lawns and trees. It may be challenging to imagine the smells of food stalls, the music, the shouts of street performers, and the chatting of crowds from all classes, entering and exiting the bath complex. The Baths of

---

3 Herodian of Antioch, Herodian of Antioch's History of The Roman Empire, Trans. Edward C. Echols (S.L.: Univ Of California Press, 2021), 3:10, 1-4)

Caracalla serviced up to 8,000 patrons a day and, near the Circus Maximus, was one of the busiest areas. What is most striking, walking towards the entrance, is just how big this complex was. Built to a height of 40 meters (130 feet), and covering an area of over 100,000 meters (over 1 million square feet), the architecture dwarfs the ancient citizen and modern visitor. It makes a statement about the stone arms of the empire, holding and embracing all who enter.

Emperor Pissed Off faded from my mind as I looked up at the soaring arches and thick red brick walls. I tried to imagine the massive Farnese Hercules statue, now in the archeological museum in Naples, which once stood at the entrance. Parts of this magnificent structure are all over Italy: the mosaic from the floor of the gymnasium in the Vatican Museums, the Farnese Bull, also in Naples, the Asclepius in Greece, the Column of Justice now in Florence and two huge granite basins which, fortunately, remained in Rome and can be found in Piazza Farnese. Scattered works of art, too masterful to have been kept in one place. I walked through the turnstile and looked down at the mosaics of geometric design, sea creatures, and cupids. I decided to explore the baths the way the Romans experienced them but keeping my clothes on. I made my way to the ancient changing room.

The *apodyterium*, or ancient locker room, was where visitors changed clothes or simply stripped naked. Here, as at other Roman baths, the sexes were divided, and usually, women were given the morning hours. While walking into the *apodyterium*, one notices that the incredible mosaic floor and the towering vaulted ceilings give the impression that this is only the beginning of greater things to be seen. But the reputation of the locker room was similar to a den of thieves, theft being commonplace, so any visitor who owned slaves would bring one along to watch his belongings or pay the attendant to do the same.

As I stood in that antechamber, I imagined two senators, let's call them Titus and Flavius. After a morning of reading scrolls, passing legislation, and a generous lunch, they ended up at the baths for an afternoon of relaxation, gossip, and people watching. The *apodyterium* was the great equalizer. The two men removed their senatorial robes and so became indistinguishable from any freedman or shopkeeper who visited the baths at the same hour. "I certainly hope half the senate isn't here again today," said Titus as his slave helped him remove his toga. Flavius shot him a glance to warn him not to speak so freely in public. There were, in fact, about a dozen other bathers in various stages of undress. The two put on their wooden-soled sandals and walked out of the locker room area. "To the palestra?" Flavius asked. "Indeed, perhaps the gladiators will be there!" Titus responded with a smile, "You are incorrigible, my friend! I wish there were a cohort of Amazons running, jumping, and looking for mates! But alas, the days of mixed bathing are passed," he sighed.

"What type of exercise would you like to do today?" Flavius asked. "Walk and watch, but mostly watch," Titus responded. Flavius laughed as they entered the outdoor palestra area. Gleaming marble walls and rich mosaic floors with depictions of boxers and wrestlers of every type invited visitors to participate in the sport. "I see your gladiator is here today," Flavius said, as he nodded to his left. "Oh yes, with legs like tree trunks, a chest rivaling that of Hercules… not to mention his other endowments. His presence makes visiting the palestra worth it," Titus stated. The senators stopped to watch as the gladiator and a companion engaged in a wrestling match. "But this is boring for you, my friend," Titus said. "No, I can admire the sport while you admire something else," he replied, smiling. Just then, another senator arrived, greeting both men. "Felix!" Flavius greeted him as Titus shifted his eyes away from the gladiator. "What a fine day it is! How are you? Your wife and family?" Flavius asked. Felix, a heavy-set middle-aged man with a red friendly face, leaned on the railing. "The sun is shining; the gods are smiling on us, and wife and sons are well. And how are you two today? Are you exercising intensely?" he asked, with a smile. Titus and Flavius laughed. "And your wives? Families?" Felix continued. "My wife continues to complain that I spend too much time at the baths," Titus began, "but that is the price of being the wife of a senator. After all, if I did not come here every day, how would I know what people are thinking and saying?" Both Felix and Titus nodded. "And you, Flavius?" Felix asked. "The same; my wife complains but is content, and I am content, yet I complain!" he replied, as all three laughed. "Well, I will let you two get back to your walk. Farewell!" Felix said as he continued on his way. "Well, now I can get back to...." Titus began, as he turned back towards the palestra court. He shook his head; the gladiator was gone.

"To the *caldarium?*" Flavius asked. There were a series of pools of various temperatures at the baths, the *caldarium* being the hottest. Titus nodded, and they soon entered a richly decorated, light-filled room with floors and pools heated by furnaces tended by unseen slaves below. The men slipped off their sandals and waded into the pool, where hundreds of other bathers were already present. The waters were more for soaking than swimming, and soon the two senators found their corner from which the entire pool area was visible. Flavius looked up at the enormous open-air windows and marble-covered walls with dozens of niches that held life-size statues of gods and emperors. "Awww, the ego of our emperor!" Flavius exclaimed. Titus shushed him; "Remember, we were not going to speak of *him!*" "Well, who shall we speak of, then?" Flavius answered. Titus looked around. "What about him?" he asked, nodding in the direction of senator Atticus, soaking on the other side of the pool. Flavius laughed and responded: "Shall we speak of his politics, daily visits to the brothel, his wife, who hates him or his sons who are thieves?" "So many topics and so little time," Titus responded. "We do have time for one story," Flavius began; "Just yesterday a reliable source told me...."; and so the two senators enjoyed exchanging gossip about their sometime friend and all-time colleague Atticus, who lay in the pool, eyes closed, indifferent to all around him.

There were three levels of heat at the baths, and soon the two made their way to the crowded and noisy *tepidarium,* a pool where the water was lukewarm, the room was smaller, and the noise echoed from the ceilings. There was more splashing and chatter in this room, which was not the type of behavior that Flavius and Titus were accustomed to, or even approved of; everyone was equal here, stripped down to their essence. Though Titus wished he could tell the freedman next to him to speak more softly, he realized that he didn't have the right. After being splashed in the face three times, Titus signaled to Flavius, and the two got out of the water and their sandals click-clocked on the mosaic floors until they reached the largest room, the *frigidarium*, where the water was cool, and the ceilings soared above the hundreds of bathers. "Aren't you going to get a massage and cleansed today?" Flavius asked as the two climbed down into the water. "Yesterday, that slave on duty poured gobs of oil on me and scraped my back so hard that it was raw! I should have him flogged!" Titus complained. "I need to heal! You?" Flavius shook his head. "Being rubbed with oil, scraped, massaged, then back in the pools: it takes me a day to recover! Then my wife complains: 'When you come home you just want to sleep!' Well, she is right. Bathing and spending time with you, my friend is enough for today," he concluded.

This room also had marble walls, niches with many statues, fountains on either side, and a ceiling that seemed to soar to the heavens. There was a section of the bath complex reserved for sunbathers, and Flavius, growing chilly in the water, took his leave of Titus to warm up while the latter remained in the pool. There were men of all ages, ethnicities, statues, and body types; Titus enjoyed looking at all of them but preferred to speak to none. When he spotted another senator on the other side, Titus turned away. When a freedman near him splashed him accidentally and apologized, he didn't respond. Titus was beginning to grow bored when Flavius returned. Getting back into the water, he approached his friend with a smile. "What are you up to?" Titus asked. Flavius laughed, then shared in a low voice: "I found your gladiator, taking in the sun, sprawled all over the ground, muscles glistening with sweat and sunlight." Titus shook his head and responded, "I may be a senator, but I am no fool. You want me to go over there, don't you? Then you want to see me speak with him, or attempt to. Then you want to see him turn over and completely ignore me. After that, you want to see me standing there, mouth agape, looking around to see who observed my humiliation. Then, and finally, you want to see me slink back here and hear me lying about the new friendship I have with this man. Well, the answer is 'no', I am not interested!" His friend was still smiling. "You are the incorrigible one!" Titus said as he playfully splashed water on his friend. "Well, you had your chance," he said, as he splashed back.

They had now been at the baths for hours and were starting to get hungry. There was a restaurant within the complex, but there were also dozens of food stalls outside, where many milled around watching the street performers, having dinner "al fresco"[4] while spending time with friends until the sun went down. "It is still early to eat; we will be hungry again later," Flavius said. Titus felt his stomach as if measuring his hunger. "Shall we spend time in the open pool before dining, then?" he asked Flavius. The man nodded.

The two came to the *natatio*, or massive outdoor swimming pool, where bathers often concluded their visit. The water was clear and crisp, fountains on all four sides, and, though crowded, the noise level was considerably lower since it was not in an enclosed room. "This time, I am leaving you briefly, for the sauna. But please come, if you wish," Titus said. "I will be here when you return, my friend," Flavius responded, as he floated towards the center of the pool.

"Greetings, salve Flavius," came a loud, high-pitched voice that roused the senator from his slumber. Opening one eye, Flavius saw Sextus, a fellow senator who frequented those baths daily, standing a few feet away from him, smiling. Standing up, Flavius greeted the man and invited him to float next to him. "Awww, the benevolence of our beloved emperor!" Sextus exclaimed as his eyes scanned the marble walls and many statues.

---

4 Outside, literarily "in the fresh air".

"Caracalla?" Flavius asked, bewildered. "Certainly Caracalla, or Marcus Aurelius Severus Antoninus Augustus, if we are to use his official name. He had all this built for the comfort of his people, he gave citizenship to all freedmen, and he even raised the pay of our soldiers, thus keeping the empire safe!" But Flavius disagreed. "Do not quote me on this, for I will deny that I ever said it. These baths were planned and initiated by Caracalla's father, perhaps knowing how unpopular his son would be. Don't forget that it is said that he killed his brother. Secondly, he only gave citizenship away so he could increase tax revenue. Third, he raised the pay of soldiers while neglecting other needs in the empire because he understands that if he controls the military, he controls everything. Your benevolence towards the emperor has benefitted you much, Sextus; I, and many others, see these things differently." Sextus was just opening his mouth to respond when Flavius added: "But let us not argue here; let us enjoy these magnificent surroundings and a moment of peace and friendship." Sextus smiled. "Indeed," he responded.

Eventually, Sextus floated away, and Titus returned. Entering the pool to cool off, he approached Flavius. "I am famished, the sun is going down, and the baths are beginning to empty. What do you say if we get dinner together?" Without a word, Flavius made his way out of the pool as his stomach growled, put on his wooden sandals, and walked towards the locker room. Titus laughed as he followed him. "Someone else is hungry too," he said, as they entered. "You may return home," Titus said to his slave guarding their belongings. "Tell my wife that I will arrive shortly," he continued. The slave made a slight bow and departed.

The sky was a golden hue as the two friends exited the baths and walked towards the food vendors, who were busily serving up take away meals for the many on their way home. The smells of grilled fish with *garum* sauce[5], roasting meats, bubbling lentil soup, and baking cheese filled the air. Flavius' stomach growled

---

5 Garum was a fish sauce popular in Ancient Rome, which was made from fermented fish, often with a strong odor and flavor.

again loudly. "Why do we not gather our food and watch the street entertainers?" Titus suggested. "Excellent idea. I am longing for some roasted fish, olives, and bread, with a large glass of cheap wine," Flavius responded. "That sounds just perfect." The two found the stall selling their fish dinner with wine and, gathering their food, walked over to the area where the street acrobats were performing. Balancing their dinner and their wine was no easy task, but the two managed to consume and drink, passing their cups back and forth. They found themselves in a crowd of about fifty people watching acrobats who wore some articles imitating gladiatorial dress. They jumped and flipped and ran in a mock battle with one another. The crowd was mesmerized as Flavius looked around. "Ummmmm," he began, catching Flavius' eye. "Your gladiator is here," he continued, motioning with his eyes. Looking over, Titus saw the dark-skinned, bearded muscular fighter dressed in a brown tunic on the other side of the crowd, his eyes fixed on the street show. Both senators found themselves staring, one out of curiosity, the other from lust. A woman suddenly approached the gladiator; she had dark brown wavy hair which she wore to her shoulders, her eyes glowed green, and her figure rivaled that of Venus. The gladiator looked at her, smiled, and took her hand; they both then turned to watch the show. "There is your Amazon!" Titus teased Flavius. "And there goes your gladiator!" Flavius responded. "Indeed! What a waste!" Titus responded. Both men laughed.

As the dusk turned to darkness and torches began to be lit in the vicinity, the two friends bid farewell. "My wife will disown me should I remain longer," Flavius said. "As will mine, if she hasn't already!" Titus responded. "Until tomorrow, my friend," Titus said. "Until tomorrow," Flavius replied.

Wandering through the streets of Rome today, street performers carry on the ancient tradition, some more eloquently than others. There is the opera singer in Piazza del Pantheon, wooing crowds by his loud trembling voice. The painted up and costumed "statues" in Piazza Navona, who try not to flinch in the hope of receiving a few coins (I always feel sorry for these people since they generate little interest and so don't make much). There are street musicians, playing everything from violins to garbage can lids, many of whom manifest considerable talent. There are the Brazilian acrobats who seem to be performing more out of fun and exhibitionism than need. The clowns, who improvise, make fun of and involve the beloved tourists are a staple feature in several piazzas and are usually very funny. There is the fire breathing woman in Trastevere, the costumed gladiators in front of the Victor Emmanuel monument, cartoonists, painters, fortune tellers, and singers: all of them being part of one grand, beautiful fantastic show that is Rome.

But what about the spray paint artists? Ahhhhh, the spray paint artists who, for some reason that I have never understood, gather the largest crowds. I become curious when I see a large crowd gathered around a street performer, and I often approach to see who is doing what. When I see the group gazing down at someone spraypainting circles and spheres on cardboard, I look at the painter, then at the crowd, and ask myself: "Am I missing something?" Maybe it is the toxic fumes that keep the group mesmerized? Looking down the street, I spot another street performer playing the most moving rendition of Vivaldi's Four Seasons that I have ever heard, with no onlookers, and here there are thirty looking at a guy spray painting cardboard. What gives?

Besides parodying the ruling class, street performers in Ancient Rome (*ludii triviales*) performed slapstick and poetry. They were so favored by the emperor Augustus that he would invite them to perform at his dinner parties.[6] According to Suetonius in *The Divine Augustus*, the emperor enjoyed inviting street comedians (itinerant humorists) to enliven the company (74.1).

Later on, the Roman satirist Juvenal (50-127 CE) described

---

6 Christopher Francese, Ancient Rome in So Many Words (New York: Hippocrene Books, 2007), page 63.

conditions in Rome which appalled him so much, including the street performers:

*I prefer even the barren island Prochyta to the Subura; for what do we see so wretched, so solitary, that you would not believe that the fires, the constant collapse of tenement roofs, and the thousand dangers of the savage city, not to mention the poets reciting in the heat of August, would frighten you worse?* (Juvenal, Satire 3:5-9).[7]

Marcus Valerius Martialis (38-102 AD) had no affection for street poets, writing that:

*You wonder why no people pay you heed?*
*Well, I'll unveil the mystery—you read.*
*Incessantly you foist on us your rhymes,*
*a legendary peril of our times.*
*No mother tiger snarling near her cubs,*
*no snake attacking us despite our clubs,*
*no scorpion paralyzingly come near,*
*can deal us such humiliating fear*
*as you, in undeterr'd reciting mode*
*producing endless drivel by the load. . .*

(Marcus Valerius Martialis, Epigram 3.44).[8]

We gather from the ancient sources that street entertainment in Ancient Rome included political parodies, comedy and skits, poetry, and singing. According to Juvenal and Martialis, much of the street poetry in Rome was terrible, described as "frightening" or "drivel." Other ancient sources describe poetry and storytelling as an art form, often combined with music and dancing (*Libanius, Defense on Behalf of Dancers*). Libanius was from Antioch but described the storytelling combined with music and dancing as an art form spread throughout the ancient world. In his Defense,

7 Juvenal, The Satires of Juvenal Translated: With Explanatory and Classical Notes, Relating to the Laws and Customs of the Greeks and Romans, trans. Thomas Sheridan (New York: AMS Press, 1978).
8 Martial and Garry Wills, Martial's Epigrams: A Selection (London: Penguin Books, 2009).

Libanius wrote about the songs, chorus, and dancers, which convey a story about gods and men (*Defense on Behalf of Dancers*, 86-90).[9]

From the emperor's dining room to the crime-ridden Subura, street entertainers have formed an intimate part of Roman life for thousands of years and were as controversial then as today. An art form? Glorified begging? Vulgar? Cool, ridiculous, amazing, deplorable, magnificent, bothersome, sad, mesmerizing, phony, funny, and entertaining! What is fascinating is that today's street entertainers are part of a long tradition that stems back to the founding of Rome and beyond, through which the spectators get to forget, if even for a few minutes, whatever burdens them and live in another world.

---

9 Margaret E. Molloy, Libanius and the Dancers (Hildesheim: Olms-weidmann, 1996).

# Chapter 3
# Artists and Performers on the Streets of Rome

What are the stories behind the street artists and performers in Rome? What choices have those persons made that led them to dance, play music, or sell paintings on the street for coins? Is it from necesity that this musician is playing for donations, or that this flamethrower is tossing up her torches, or that this artist is selling his paintings for a fraction of what they would cost in a shop?

I wondered about the stories of these street performers in Rome; I went to Piazza Navona and tried to speak with the Charlie Chaplin impersonator and his musician friends about their background. They demanded 100 euros to chat with me, however, so I walked away. But I found others eager to tell their stories.

- **Tell me your story.**

"My name is Federica Tranchida (The Sparkle)[10] and I am 35 years old. My artistic expression consists of fire dancing, but recently I have branched out into comedy."

"My name is Ann Louise Amendolagine[11], I am 66 years old, and I tap dance on the streets of Rome."

---

10 https://www.thesparklefire.com
11 www.facebook.com/ann.amendolagine

"My name is Antonio, but I am known as Jonathan; I am 81 years old, and I have been a street artist since I was a child."

**Sparkle.** "About 13 years ago, on a day like many others, an old schoolmate of mine asked me: 'Can you be my stand-in for my fire shows when I cannot make it?' I didn't know what to expect, but I was ready to dive into something new and unknown. My answer was affirmative. That 'yes' changed my life."

**Ann.** "My first dancing lesson was at age 20, and I was told that I wasn't built for it: I was flat-footed, thick ankled, and pigeon-toed! Others told me that it was impossible to carve out a career in dancing, especially for me. I pursued dance anyway because, from the first moment, I felt an incredible joy and love when I danced. I only became a street performer out of desperation, and I had no idea how to begin or where to go to learn or how to collect money, so I just started dancing on a small street in Rome to see what would happen.

"Many street artists watch out for each other, and, during this initial stage, three street performers coached and advised me just when I was getting discouraged. They were like my guardian angels. The first was Evi, a man who sold his paintings in the piazzas of Rome. He approached and urged me to move my act to Piazza Navona, which I thought was way out of my league. 'No, you're good; go for it!' he said. He arranged that I could dance in front of his friend's restaurant in the piazza and, in 2003, I performed in Piazza Navona for the first time. But when I wasn't getting any tips, I grew discouraged. One day another street performer, dressed as Charlie Chaplin, saw me crying; he came up to me and said: 'It is not enough for you to perform. You have to develop a technique to get tips!' He suggested that I approach the tables with my hat so patrons could tip without getting out of their seats. And, surprisingly, this worked, and I started to make money through tips! The third guardian angel was a Russian man selling paintings on the streets of Rome. He watched my routines, and one day, pulling me aside, said: 'What you do is so valuable, and it is so clear that you are a professionally trained dancer. But I would suggest that you do not stick to a set pattern of dance, but you get closer to people so that they can see your eyes and smile. You will see a difference.' I followed his advice, and he was right."

**Jonathan.** "My story begins in 1972. I was walking in Piazza Navona and I passed this church, St. Mary of Peace, nearby. This church was neglected and in a mess, and I felt pity for it. There was a sign nearby on a building that read 'for rent,' so I rented it and used it as an artist studio within sight of this neglected church. So I had a room, I created a fireplace, and there I painted. Friends and young people came to visit to keep warm around the fire and watch me paint. It was only one room, but we realized there was a basement underneath at a certain point. We knocked through the floor and discovered an ample space full of trash. There, in that space, I created a restaurant that became known as *La Focaccia*[12]; in 1982, I had 45 tables outside and 15 Swedes working for me. With the restaurant's success, we were able to clean up and restore the church and space around it, transforming it into a place people wanted to visit. Keep in mind that people used this area to inject drugs, there was a lot of crime, and it was filthy. Today it is full of plants and flowers and is completely transformed. This work we did must have saved some people's lives. This is one of the most satisfying things I have accomplished in my life.

"The restaurant was beautiful; since I never completed high school, my American wife became interested in

---

12 http://1stmuse.com/focaccia/index-i.htm

managing the restaurant; we had two children together. My daughter lives in San Francisco, and my son lives here in Rome. Things didn't work out between myself and my wife; we separated, and then the restaurant fell apart. But I found another opportunity right away, and I started Jonathan Pub, which became famous all over the world.

"After this, I found a place owned by some German priests and I rented it and turned it into another pub which became very popular, which was called "Jonathan's Angels" but now is called "Mons"[13]. There was a courtyard where there was an ancient washing basin; rather than remove it, I restored it to its original state. When I was finished restoring the building, I stood back and threw a coin in that basin, just like the Trevi Fountain. Imagine how many coins were tossed into that water basin over the years! This is famous, called *Jonathan's Basin*. Twenty-four million coins were tossed into that basin! Actors, celebrities, and politicians came to visit.

"In 2006, the German priests didn't renew my lease, so we had to close down. I returned to being a painter in Piazza Navona; after 50 years, they evicted us, so now I don't have that work. Now I am in Piazza San Simeone where I come to visit my friends, and I sell a few paintings."

### • What type of street entertainment do you do?

**Sparkle.** "My show consists of dancing with fire. We have recently also introduced a comedy show in collaboration with my partner."

**Ann.** "I sing and tap dance to recorded music. I clown around and dance with children and grown-ups alike. I have a dog-petting station, starring my dog Ginger Rogers, free of charge to anyone and everyone in need of some puppy love. I sing pop songs, love songs, jazz standards,

13 https://www.monscrew.com

blues, reggae, and rock ballads. I sing songs in English, Italian, French, and Spanish. I am also a point of reference for all the street people that see me. Together we make sure we are not forgotten and that we are not invisible."

**Jonathan.** "I am an artist, painting, and sculpture. I used to paint in the style of French impressionism, but I eventually found my own way. Today tourists are not willing to pay for a painting for what it is worth. When prices came down, we had to go to Naples to look for artists, and some started buying paintings from China to sell in the piazza. I left this work when I could no longer sell my paintings.

"Many of my paintings are huge, taller than 2 meters, and painted on canvas or wood. Today my style is modern and uniquely my own, and most of my paintings I give away as gifts.

"I used to be able to sell French impressionist paintings for 300-400 euros; I also used to create lots of paintings of the Virgin Mary. I've also sculpted in tufa stone, but now my wrist is injured, so I cannot do this."

- **Why Rome?**

**Sparkle.** "In 2013, when I lived in Bergamo, a friend from school came to stay with me.

An immediate friendship began between myself and this schoolmate. The following year I went to see him in Rome, and I ended up staying for three months; during this time, I performed in Campo de Fiori, Piazza Trilussa, and Piazza Navona."

**Ann.** "Because Rome is a place where people can find me. Because in Rome it doesn't rain at all some months and hardly at all in others. Because Rome has vast pedestrian areas. Because Rome is impossible to police completely… yet. Because everyone is happy when they are eating ice cream and strolling around Rome. Because Rome was conceived as the center of the universe and a multinational city. Because the colors of Rome are like nowhere else I've ever seen. Because Rome is a place that everyone will come to at least once. Because it is endlessly beautiful."

- **If you could choose any career, what would it be?**

**Sparkle.** "Perhaps I would choose any career compatible with my abilities, as long as I could live a peaceful life. I can't imagine my life without art! On stage, I feel at ease; I couldn't live without creating, together with the study and the commitment necessary to build new routines and shows. It is difficult to explain the adrenaline and emotions that I feel during a performance."

**Ann.** "If I could choose any career, I would still choose the one I am in now, as a dancer, but in recent years, this has expanded to singing, and I derive the same happiness from singing as I do from dancing. But I would give up the street for a real job with a real contract. I dream of going to work every day, warming up, doing hair, and makeup, doing charity events, and having a real stable life. In the 1980s, I had this life, dancing in large productions in Las Vegas: two shows a night, one day off a week. I believe this could happen again. My only doubt is: would I be happy if my dreams come true? So many of them already have come true, yet I find myself fighting to be happy in the life I have now."

**Jonathan.** "I value my freedom, and I never wanted to work in an office or an institution. One of the most beautiful things we did was opening *Jonathan's Angels*. We made an impact in that once crime-ridden neighborhood; some people have sought me out to thank me for creating that locale that helped transform the area around Santa Maria della Pace. I've been told that I saved them from a life of addiction because we were able to transform that space."

- **What is the hardest thing about your life?**

**Sparkle.** "The hardest thing about my life is probably my job! It is as beautiful as it is difficult and complex. It requires a lot of energy spent in training, creating new shows, relationships with suppliers, updating the website, cultivating a presence on social media, finding new customers, secretary work, finding and buying new equipment, and maintaining old equipment. After all this, it is not certain that an artist can even make money from the show. Sometimes my tip hat, after a show, is empty! Very often you work 100 hours and perhaps collect 20 or 40 euros. Grit, optimism, and perseverance are essential to moving forward."

**Ann.** "It is difficult not knowing if there will be a place for me to perform on the street because of other buskers locking me out. It is a hard feeling and can be isolating; I pay the price of not being political and not dishonest with my work. It is difficult to deal with the physical pain and exhaustion of performing on the street, not having a dressing room or sound technician or stagehand or chauffeur. Facing the never-ending bills is scary. Living in a foreign language and always be considered a foreigner because I have an accent is something I deal with daily."

**Jonathan.** "What made me suffer most was when my American wife left, and my business and family fell apart. During that time, there were lots of impoverished young people in this area who used to wait for me in Piazza Navona, and we would spend time together as I sold my paintings. I remember a musician who played for us when he saw a group of us together, which made us very happy.

"Now I have arrived at a point where I cannot afford the rent for the house I am in, and I can no longer sell paintings in Piazza Navona because a law was passed restricting artists. But somehow, I will get through this also."

• **What is the best thing about your life?**

**Sparkle.** "To be able to do what makes me happy."

**Ann.** "My fantastic dog. Music, dancing, and singing. Interacting with children and making people smile, reaching many of my goals. Having a patio garden and watching things grow. Being Italian."

**Jonathan.** "I have a lot of history in Rome. I have always tried to love those who have come into my life."

• **What would you change about your life if you could?**

**Sparkle.** "I would go to live in a place that can offer more job opportunities. A place with more stimuli and is dynamic and welcoming."

**Ann.** "My dream is to settle in New York, realize a body of work and have greater energy and less fatigue."

**Jonathan.** "Everything was a beautiful choice, and I am grateful for all of it. Founding the pub gave me a sense of joy, creating work for so many people and transforming the neighborhood. What made me feel bad was when my lease was not renewed, but that was not in my power."

• **Are there days when you cannot get enough to eat?**

**Sparkle.** "No, luckily, we can eat every day, but we are very thrifty. Unfortunately, in the past, we have gone through very, very difficult times…"

**Ann.** "I am a street performer who earns only what ends up in my hat after my performance. Others also sell CDs of their music or DVDs of their performance. Selling anything while busking is illegal, but if it is 'offered' and the price is only 'suggested,' it can be overlooked. It is costly to live in the city, and every penny I earn goes to paying rent, electricity, gas, condo, transportation, and telephone. I shop for food and cook for myself and my dog. Sometimes, we go hungry when I don't have time to go shopping or because I'm so tired that I can't find the energy to prepare our meal."

**Jonathan.** "No, I don't go hungry. I have friends!"

• **If you could live anywhere, where would it be and why?**

**Sparkle.** "Where I don't know. I would love to live in a different place other than the current one, but I don't have a clear idea where! I would like to live in a place where artists are valued and appreciated, a society capable of understanding how much effort and perseverance are necessary to carry out this work in the best possible way."

**Ann.** "I would choose to live in a beautiful place, maybe in France, near the sea, but close to cultural activity and full of natural beauty. Most likely not in the US. Someday I will begin my journey to find this place that I long for."

**Jonathan.** "I would only live in Rome, surrounded by my history and those I care about."

• **What are your hopes and dreams?**

**Sparkle.** "I dream of bringing my shows around the world. I hope that my passion, enthusiasm, commitment, and tenacity are recognized and appreciated."

**Ann.** "My greatest and most ambitious dream is to get a job in a Broadway show, in a show that people love, that runs for another 20 years, in a part that people will remember, with a cast that doesn't fight and where there is a spiritual bond of friendship and fellowship. Or else, I'd like to get into a company of the PostModern Jukebox; I think a woman who sings and tapdances and is over 65 years old is a fantastic gimmick and could have a lot of appeal. I would like to belong to something I could give my all, be a part of something, and be cherished and valued as an artist. With less chaos and crisis in my life, I could help others who are in difficulty, instead of being the one who needs help."

**Jonathan.** "I have a little business now with my friend Paolo to sell some paintings. As far as my love life, I am better single; I've had many women in my life, but I like my freedom. I live alone, and I like this. What I lack is finding a little more work to make ends meet. I hope we can expand our reach into selling more paintings so that I can make enough to pay my rent. My dream would be to open a small artist studio, sell some paintings, and make a living in this last part of my life."

- **How long have you been a street entertainer?**

**Sparkle.** "For about 13 years."

**Ann.** "I began around 2001."

**Jonathan.** "In one way or another, since I was a child."

# Chapter 4
# Tasting History

History comes alive to the extent that the senses are involved: can I see, touch, smell, hear, or even taste it? History loses its aridity when it enters into one's experience, and Rome is the world's most ideal history venue.

I had an archeology professor in Rome who had some nutty ideas, like the day he proposed that the Garden of Eden's story was validated by the discovery of snake fossils dating from around the time humans first appeared on the earth. But he had a passion for the experience of archeology. Every week he gathered his class and brought us down to explore Rome underground, starting from ancient burial areas.

As we walked down the stairs into Priscilla's catacombs, the first thing I noticed was that, with every step, the temperature was dropping. It hovers around 15 degrees Celsius (60 degrees Fahrenheit), and, being early October and still warm in Rome, I was unprepared for this temperature change. "It's cold as fuck!" one of my seminarian colleagues muttered as we made our way down. Our professor stopped us and explained that these catacombs are less visited by tourists but are relevant to scholars because of the history written in the frescoes. While he was speaking, I became aware of a musty, earthy smell, and, all around us, open empty tombs. When he paused, I asked, "Where are the bones?" He shook his head. "Grave robbers, tourists. What remained were moved below, where souvenir seekers could not take them. " The professor then encouraged us to touch the soft tufa rock and showed us how easy it could be broken or carved. As I felt the cold stone under the tomb next to me, I wondered about the person who cut that space in the second or third century and the family standing outside that tomb as their loved one's remains were sealed up.

We continued along the tunnels until we entered a space that our professor introduced as the Greek Chapel. When he turned on the lights, my 21-year-old mouth dropped. The first thing I saw was a praying figure on the white ceiling, surrounded by mysterious shapes. The hands were raised in prayer rather than folded, as was the custom in the ancient world. As we turned to look at every nook and cranny of that old chapel, our professor pointed straight up and asked us to look more closely. We bent our heads back as we gazed at the figure of the good shepherd surrounded by, what appeared to be, two sheep. Our teacher put his fingers on his lips to silence our whispering; the soft tufa seemed to absorb any lingering sounds, and he let the silence last for a full minute, as he pointed to his ear to signal the intense silence that surrounded us. "There are five miles of tunnels down here, so do not separate yourself and do not get lost," he said quietly. He continued in a low voice: "Now look at this fresco above your heads and tell me what you notice." We looked again and stared and wondered what he wanted us to see. "He has no beard!" someone called out. "Very good," he said. "What does that mean?" We were all silent; then, I volunteered, "It represented him when he was younger." The professor nodded. "Perhaps. The figure of a good shepherd was also used in pre-Christian iconography; it could have been adapted or reinterpreted here. Or this could be a younger Christ. Some have suggested that this is not a figure of Christ at all, so we must view it in context. Now look around this room and tell me what you see," he suggested. Soon my fellow students were calling out: *"The breaking of the bread"* and *"The adoration of the Magi"* and *"Scenes from the Old Testament"* and one called out *"Is this the Madonna and child?"*, pointing up. Our teacher seemed satisfied with our discoveries. "Yes, there is the mysterious praying woman, who was probably buried here. The stories of the old and new testaments and here, my friends, is the oldest known painting of the Madonna and child. Here is our history in paint and stone and tunnels and darkness, and cold. This is the significance of the catacombs!"

When we came out of the darkness after this experience, we felt like we were in a different world. We had seen history; we had felt the cold, we had listened to the silence; we had touched the tufa; the only sense we did not employ was taste. "Ewwwwwwwwwwww!" someone called out. "He just put his tongue on a piece of tufa!" Let me take that back; we used all five senses.

This class helped nourish my love of hands-on archeology, and, decades later, I found myself descending the stairs in St. Clement's Basilica near the Lateran in Rome; with each level, I was going back in time. The air grew colder, the smells mustier, the street sounds disappeared, and I became aware, on the lowest level, of water rushing behind a wall where there was an underground river. The Mithraic Temple was in front of me, dating from around 200 CE. There was a carving of a bull in the center; there were also rows of seating on both sides, and a trough down the center where the blood of the sacrificed bull flowed. There was a group of school children present, chatting and clamoring, but they quickly left, and my companion and I were then alone. We found an ancient seating area, carved into the stone, right outside the Mithraeum, and sat in that spot in silence, somehow feeling connected to the Roman soldiers who sat in that place before entering the Mithraeum. This was history come alive.

I like to go to the Forum at night after the crowds have

dispersed, and gates closed. I find a secluded spot overlooking the ancient area, and I listen. I lean over and begin to imagine the voices of senators and slaves, tourists and freedmen walking down the Via Sacra and side streets, marveling at the sites, going about their business, carrying the master's supplies, chatting about dinner, wondering about politics. Different languages are echoing through the Forum. I can almost hear them, and I wonder how life felt to that person walking down that road two thousand years ago. My imagination flows to the senate-house, as senators entered, or their home, once they arrived, or inside the temple, where they honored their god.

I shift my position so that I get a clear view of the House of the Vestal Virgins, and I wonder what their lives were like in that place. Were they like our modern-day nuns, dedicating their lives to their god as they kept the fire of Rome's prosperity burning? I imagine an atmosphere of silence as the Vestals chanted their prayers before their sacred images while the streets outside bustled with tourists and residents. I then look up to where the emperor himself, from the Palatine, could look down on his Vestals from his palace. He knew that all was well in the Empire if all was well in the House of the Vestals.

The emperor, meanwhile, thought about his military campaigns, the treasury, or his building programs. If he was Domitian, he might be wondering if the words of the astrologer were valid, which predicted his death at noon on September 18, 96 CE. His fear of death had become an obsession, and he had the marble walls of his palace polished so that he could see the reflection should someone try to creep up behind him. Oh Domitian, as you gaze out your window at the crowds below, little suspecting that your servants would be involved in a plot against you. You thought that you were safe when noon came and passed, so you let your guard down. But the palace lied to you about the hour; midday had just arrived as you were brought papers to sign, and Stephanus, one of your secretaries, pulled out a concealed dagger and stabbed you in the groin. More servants rushed in as they stabbed you over and over until your breath stopped. And yet here you gaze, believing that all is well because the House of the Vestals is lit from within and its fire glows still.

As I walk near the Forum on my way to my lodging, I notice the Mamertine prison and resolve to return tomorrow to experience it once more.


I had heard the story of the Mamertine when I visited Rome at age 19. It is an ancient Roman prison that held political prisoners before execution and an important site in the history of Christianity. It was honored as the place where both Saints Peter and Paul were held before their execution. When I was a young man, I believed everything our guide told us about our visited sites. Even in later years, after the historicity of the imprisonment of the Apostles in the Mamertine was called into doubt, there was something about that place that continued to move me.

The ugly baroque church above is not what attracted me to the Mamertine; it is the multitude of stories connected to that place that fascinates me. When Nathaniel Hawthorne descended the steps into the black stone dungeon, he encountered a group of pilgrims, tapers in hand, ascending the stairs; once the crowd had left, he noticed on the wall an imprint of a face where, legend says, St. Peter's visage remains. He saw it, he touched it, just as I reach in and feel it now.

As I descend to the lower level of the cell, I feel the humidity increase. Looking around, I see a dimly lit semicircle chamber, with a hole in the ceiling, covered by a grate. On one side of the room is an altar with an upside-down cross; next to it is a stone pillar and on the floor is a hole opening to an underground spring, filled with water. There is an inscription indicating that this was the place where Saints Peter and Paul were held captive before one was crucified upside down (hence the upside-down cross on the altar), and the other was beheaded. It is a gruesome place with a sad history; looking up at the circular hole, I realize that this was the only way in or out; the stairs were built for pilgrims centuries after the prison was closed. Dark, damp, cold; prisoners languished here. The story goes that Peter struck up a friendship with his Roman guards, speaking to them about his belief. Eventually, the soldiers asked to be baptized in secret, but there was no water at hand. Suddenly water began bubbling up from the floor, hence the origin of the underground spring. Peter eventually lost his life but not his belief.

As I stand in the dim light of that prison space, there is something that feels comforting. This feeling could be the result of the realization that I am standing in ancient Rome, built by hands around 616 BCE. It might be from the understanding that history happened here as the lives of those who dared to stand up to Rome's power were held in this place; it could be that the spirit of the two apostles somehow lingers still. I crouch down to rest and begin to reflect on the conviction of that man, Peter, who was just a fisherman from Galilee. He is like someone who never got on an airplane before and suddenly finds himself the pilot. But in his case, he was in prison.

What kind of man was this, I wonder. The Bible casts Peter as being more of an impulsive, affectionate man than a stubborn one, yet here he was, day after day, in this space, waiting to be killed. It makes me reflect on what is important to me, what I would be willing to sacrifice everything for, and what kind of man I am.

I left the Mamertine with these questions accompanied by a great sense of peace.

Below the overpowering Renaissance dome of St. Peter's Basilica lies a little known first-century graveyard that visitors can explore in small groups and with a reservation. The tour runs like a "Whodunit" expedition. The descending path brings viewers into the cold darkness, and the hundreds inside the Basilica above become muffled and then disappear altogether.

Walking through this necropolis below the floor of St. Peter's imparts a strange sensation; traveling along a first-century road, on each side, are mausoleums, set up as if they were shops. It becomes evident that most of these are not Christian tombs; it was a convenient burial ground outside the city walls. The first impression is that there are lots of bricks holding up the Basilica and lots of tombs. One of the first seen is the sarcophagus of a child who died at the age of 11 months, and on the other side is the tomb of the freed slave Lucius Tullius Zethus, under Hadrian's reign. Every grave has a story of hopes and sorrows and dreams. The oldest graves are the first we encounter, as the guide explains that we are slowly making our way towards the "red wall" where the tomb of St. Peter is believed to be located. "Excavations were begun in the 1940s," our guide continued, "to ascertain if there was a historical basis for the tradition that the Basilica was built on top of St. Peter's tomb, martyred under the reign of Nero, whose circus was nearby. It is believed that Peter was buried here because it was close at hand, this area being right outside the city walls at the time, which was about the year 64 CE."

We continued along our way as the feeling of claustrophobia increased, ducking into ever more elaborate tombs, until we reached one with Christian symbolism dating from perhaps the fifth century. "The increase in Christian symbolism is a clue that we are getting closer," our guide reminded us, as the path became narrower. She stopped us to explain the significance of the red wall. "It is called the 'red wall' due to the red plaster used to cover it, but the wall itself was simply put in place to separate various burial zones. When excavations uncovered this wall, they discovered that a funerary monument had been built against it, which was dated about one hundred years after Peter's death. A portion of this wall was covered with ancient graffiti, written in Greek, and one of the scrawlings on the red wall reads 'Peter is here.' This discovery was revolutionary, but archeologists immediately asked: where? Where are the remains of Peter? The archeologist Margherita Guarducci was able to study the various sets of bones found in this area. One set stood out: the remains were found in a secret repository, wrapped in purple cloth with gold thread. On further study, the bones were determined to be of a man of 60-70 years of age, 5 feet 7, and of robust constitution. The bones were mostly fragments, but scientists were able to identify them; it is noteworthy that no feet bones were found. Remember that Peter was crucified upside down and was condemned as a criminal, so it makes sense that he may have been cut down from his cross before the Christians obtained his body. Guarducci weighed this and other evidence and concluded that the bones of Peter had been found. We will now proceed to see where all this took place."

By this time, I wanted to crawl over her and get to the red wall! "We no longer bring visitors right next to the wall for its preservation, but we will see it from a short distance," she said, leading us forward. At a certain point, she stopped and pointed forward as we saw a red wall ahead between stones. She then motioned us to look at a model. "This is what you are looking at, though you have an obstructed view. The wall, the shrine, the graffiti, and the place where the remains were found," she said, pointing to parts of the glass-covered model. "We, fortunately, found some tiles behind the red wall which bear the mark of the future Emperor Marcus Aurelius, who owned the furnace where the tiles were made. This dates the wall to about 146 CE. The fact that the shrine was built around a niche in the wall demonstrates its importance in early Christianity. If you look very closely," she continued, pointing towards the wall, "you can see the scratches, the graffiti that confirmed that Peter was buried here."

This was cool; it was like a thriller that we were players in. "Where are the bones now?" one of my fellow gawkers asked. "For years, they were in a plastic box on a metal shelf in storage, but now they have been replaced where they were found," our guide affirmed.

"This is the conclusion of our tour; you are welcome to stay here a few minutes, and then we will leave up through the basilica." But I didn't want to leave; I wanted to stay in this space and continue to live this adventure. When our crowd of twelve began to move forward, I felt I was leaving part of myself in that necropolis where history had come alive again.

# Chapter 5
# Americans

I speak Italian; some would even say I am fluent. Why is it that every time I address a shopkeeper or resident in Rome in Italian, they always respond in English? Other times, even before I open my mouth, they assume that I am American. What gives me away?

I wondered about this and began a quest to observe what makes Americans stand out from other tourists visiting the city.

There is a calm and quiet atmosphere while riding the morning buses in Rome; residents tend to read, reflect, or look out the window; if they do engage in conversation, it is in low voices. One morning I traversed the city when a few tourists got on board at the stop; some got on from the back door and one from the front. The quiet, sleepy atmosphere shattered when a loud voice echoed above the passengers' heads: "SHOULD WE GET OFF ON THE NEXT STOP? WHERE IS MARGIE? SHOULD WE GO TO THE COLOSSEUM FIRST?" A conversation thus ensued, across the bus, about how they would plan their day. Since I am a tall man, it was difficult for me to sink into the crowd so as not to be seen as American. "DO YOU WANT TO GET LUNCH THERE?" The questions and banter continued, without any awareness of the noise level or presence of other passengers. All of a sudden one of them screeched, "OH MY GAWD!" Americans. Loud. The first give away.

OK, I got the loudness part down; speak softly. But why do Europeans in general, and Italians specifically, know that I am American before I speak? This will take some more observation. Perhaps begin with clothing. What do Americans wear that Italians would not touch? My quest continued on the streets of Rome, but I first asked my Italian friends for their input. "T-shirts with a university name on them; we would never wear this." "Grown men wearing baseball caps, especially when they wear them backward; what are they thinking?" "Men walking around the historical center in tank tops; always an American." "White socks. Period." "Young women wearing gobs of makeup; American tourists. They usually walk in groups." "Baggy clothes or gym clothes when they are not going to the gym. Why do Americans like clothing that is three times too big?" "Shorts when it is cold outside. Americans love their shorts. "A shirt that says something they did, like running a marathon or visiting a forest." "Americans wear sneakers everywhere; don't they have nicer shoes?"

So I looked at my traveling clothes: Harvard T-shirt. Lake Tahoe T-Shirt. U2 concert T-shirt. Black sneakers. Brown sneakers. White sneakers. White socks. Cargo shorts. Fanny pack. Cowboy hat. I can change all of these but not my cowboy hat.

Watching Americans see the Roman Forum or Colosseum for the first time reveals a sense of amazement that can be irritating on the one hand and inspiring on the other. Europeans are used to ancient monuments, historical buildings, and archaic statues and can be jaded. But standing on the Via Sacra as Americans look up at the Arch of Titus, and hearing "This is AWESOME!" and "I can't believe we are here!" reveals a particular American capacity to be astounded by the artifacts of history. Could I be showing my Americanism as I stand in the middle of St. Peter's Basilica, with head thrown back, gawking at the dome as I walk in circles, muttering to myself, "This is soooooo cool!"? Or when I go out to the Via Appia on a Sunday, when the road is closed to traffic, lie down on the exposed Roman road to take selfies with the 2,000-year-old chariot tracks? Wow, that was awesome!

Americans often consume food in function of activities and energy, especially while traveling, and are sometimes unused to the lingering meals prevalent in Italy. Watching the crowds surge in and out of the Trevi Fountain area, periodically, I notice groups of 2 or 3 eating while walking, pausing, then continuing, drink in one hand, food in the other, munching along the way. Rome is full of American chompers during the day, eager to see and do as much as possible. It is not surprising that, while balancing a dripping pizza slice and coca-cola, the Italian response to the American's "Buon giorno" is always "Good morning."

But how do waiters always know when an American is sitting at a table, even before any words are exchanged? I asked a waiter at a restaurant just off Piazza Navona to share his experience. "I know they are Americans if they are surprised when I do not bring them ice water, and they are even more surprised to find that they have to pay for bottled water. When someone asks to drink tap water, I don't care what language they are trying to speak; I know they are Americans. Another clue is when a customer orders french fries; Italians eat french fries also. But here, they come in, they sit down, and the ONLY thing they order is french fries. I ask: do you want some pasta? Do you want some meat? No, only french fries. I also know the customer is American if, when I serve them a beer, rather than pouring it into the glass that I provided, they drink it directly from the bottle. Oh, and one more thing: an American asks for the 'restroom'; when I ask them if they want the toilette, they seem offended."

An American trait that I have noticed in restaurants and elsewhere in Rome is that we Americans tend to compare everything to the United States. One afternoon, for example, I was in a cafe near the Pantheon with a friend enjoying a cappuccino (which also gave me away as American) with a pastry; at a certain point, a handsome American couple walked in and spoke to the barista in English. "I would like a coffee," the woman said. The barista looked perplexed, and asked her in broken English: "What type of coffee? Espresso? Cappuccino? Americano?"

The woman insisted, "A coffee!" The barista looked at her and waited for clarification. Then, in an irritated tone, she said: "A NORMAL coffee!" He looked down and began preparing her an Americano. I sat a few tables away from a man dining alone at another restaurant, berating the waitress about his pasta. "This isn't even cooked!" he said. The waitress said: "But it is cooked *al dente*[14]; if you wish, I can bring you something else." The man shook his head. "Back home, they know how to cook pasta! I just want the bill. No food!" The waitress looked upset and hesitated, wanting to make good for the customer. He sat there, shaking his head until she left. Using the US as a measure is an American trait that is not the most endearing.

Americans are an excitable people, and American tourists become very enthusiastic when they meet other Americans abroad. Step onto a bus in Rome, and one often hears a conversation such as this: "You're from Michigan, too? That's AMAZING! Who would think that we would meet someone else from our home state here? Where do you live? You're KIDDING! I grew up in Grand Rapids, and my sister still lives there. I can't believe this! Do you know Katie Smith? She is my sister and works at Stocking Elementary School, 2nd grade. How long are you in Rome for?...." Americans abroad tend to seek to bond with other Americans and look for any link from the past or present to help them feel that this new acquaintance is a relative or friend. Of course, they are neither, but for a moment, it almost feels like they are; another American trait.

The monologue on ancestry is an American activity that I have been guilty of. "On my father's side, my grandfather was from Slovenia and grandmother from Czechoslovakia, but her town was part of Hungary. Of course, the area is now Slovakia, after Czech separated. Now on my mother's side, my ancestry is quite different…" I have chattered on, little aware of whether my audience was engaged or not. I have seen this play out in Rome, as a friendly American traces his Italian ancestral line

---

14 Firm to the bite.

from grandfather to great grandfather as the waiter listening is just trying to take the orders. For some reason, Americans believe that Italians are interested that their great grandfather was from Bari or their grandmother from Sicily, and are especially ready to engage strangers in tracing their Italian ancestry.

But after I had all this down: I put away my cowboy hat, dressed European style, no running shoes, and kept the fanny pack in the suitcase; when I went out in Rome, the locals still addressed me in English before I opened my mouth. I asked an Italian friend of mine, how everyone still knows I am American?! He said: "Because you are smiling." Oh, the betrayal of the smile! This calls for further observation.

I went out to wander the streets of Rome, looking for smiles, researching what provoked them, with whom they were shared, and how often they were given. It only took a few hours wandering around the historical center that I was able to make my first conclusions. In general, Italians in Rome don't smile at strangers but readily laugh, carouse, and smile within their groups. On the other hand, Americans smile when they go into a shop, ask a stranger a question or pay for their bill at a restaurant, they smile! I find myself smiling as I walk through the streets of Rome because I am so happy to be here, and when I address a shopkeeper or barista, I smile because I am thinking that I am so lucky to be chatting with someone who lives in this incredible place! Will our smiles continue to give us away as Americans? Perhaps it is worth it.

# Chapter 6
# Eating

I am no foodie. That's not to say that I don't enjoy a great meal, but I am not the type to research the best restaurants. But experience has taught me a few things about finding great food in Rome and avoiding the mediocre.

My first rule of thumb is to avoid eating in dense tourist areas. These restaurants thrive more on geography than food quality and are well aware that they will never see most patrons again. Sometimes merely walking a few blocks out of the main tourist thoroughfares reaps the benefits of better food that locals trust.

There is a street near the Vatican where many tourists end up after their morning visit: Borgo Pio, lined with shops and outdoor restaurants. Even seasoned travelers get tired and sit down at the nearest restaurant, as I did that Saturday afternoon. I knew better, but I did it anyway: pasta please, followed by the main dish. When the pasta came, I realized that it had been frozen and then microwaved, since some parts of it were chewy and dry, resulting from microwave cooking. The meat dish was the same, so I ate a few bites, swallowed a few pieces of bread, and, after paying my bill, made my way out of that neighborhood, resolving to not eat on that street again.

On another day, I was in the area of St. John Lateran, hungry as usual but unwilling to settle for a mediocre meal. I purposely set out on the side streets, away from tourists, and stepped into a plain-looking restaurant full of Italians. The restaurant lacked the street hawkers who try to entice you to choose their establishment; the waiter said: "Prego" when I entered, showing me to a table. I ordered the pasta, which was some of the best I have eaten in Rome; I then ordered a beef stew (*spezzatino di manzo*), which was incredible, and paid less than I had near the Vatican. My rule of thumb paid off.

Traveling on a teacher's salary forced me to be creative to make my money last, and soon I discovered Rome's Happy Hour opportunities. If I could diminish the cost of one meal a day, my money would last longer. With this in mind, I stepped into a cafe in Campo dei Fiori and spied the buffet on the bar. Glancing around, I read that one glass of wine for 5 euros (it is 10 euros today) would entitle the patron to access the buffet. This could work, but I had to limit myself to one glass!

I ordered my wine, got 5 sandwiches (they were small), and proceeded to make a meal out of this experience. I had to drink tiny sips to make the wine last throughout my food gathering. I was still hungry; eyeing my half glass of wine and the buffet bar, I laid my shame aside and got 3 more sandwiches with a few small slices of pizza. "Would you like another glass?" the waitress asked me as I ate my last sandwich. "No, thank you," I said with my mouth stuffed; after all, I still had some wine left! I was still hungry. After some hesitation, I got up and slinked my way to the buffet to load up my next plate.

Stomach full, I paid 5 euros and walked out of the cafe. I felt embarrassed but satisfied that I found a way to stay within budget.

When I told my friend about the incident afterward, he suggested that the next time I go there, I would probably see a photograph of myself posted on the cafe's wall, with the circle-backslash symbol over my face.

Another little known budget-friendly eating practice in Rome is to buy lunch at the Pontifical Universities. Ever since I lived in Rome, the Gregorian University, near the Trevi Fountain, had the reputation of having the best coffee bar. Since that time, the bar evolved into a full-fledged cafeteria. Years later, I remembered this as I strode through the front doors, acting as if I owned the place. Not wanting to explain to the porter that I was searching for a cheap meal, I headed directly for the *GregCafe*, which was full of priests and religious sisters. The menu posted outside said that one could have pasta, entree, bread, water, and dessert for 9.5 euros! Ten minutes later, I devoured my *penne arrabbiata*, followed by my chicken cutlet, salad, and bread roll amidst the chatty Gregorian professors and students. The food was hardy, fresh, and the portions were generous. Since then, I have returned here every time I visit Rome; the proprietors soon recognized me and urged me to try their spin-off restaurant just down the street, which I promised that I would do.

This newly opened restaurant, *Sphaeristerium Ristobar*, near the Gregorian University, had no outdoor seating, but when I walked inside, I found another world. Clean, tastefully decorated, with a bakery and coffee bar on the street level and the restaurant below, I was impressed. The waitstaff was courteous but not pushy like other restaurants; I sat down, was given a menu, and saw that the prices were reasonable with a wide variety of selections. "Pane e aqua per favore[15]"; the bread proved to be the best I had in Rome, and when I ordered a chicken dish, skipping the pasta, the servings were so generous that I didn't hunger for more. I found a gold mine of food. But why was the food so incredible, the service so discreet and the ambiance so amazing, and yet it was not even half full? "We do not have an outside seating area," my waiter explained, "so we draw our customers with the quality of our food." I nodded and agreed. Could it be that the flashier restaurants with outdoor seating in the tourist zones did not have to be as concerned about the quality of their food because they did not rely on return customers? But the restaurants on more isolated streets, where Italians frequented, found it essential to keep the quality up since word of mouth drove their business?

I wondered what the story was behind this restaurant, so I

---

15 "Bread and water, please."

asked to meet the owner, a man named Francesco. I returned the next day when he was less busy to hear his story. His words drew me into his world.

- **Francesco, what is the history of *Sphaeristerium Ristobar* evolving from the *GregCafe*?**

"*GregCafe* started like a bet because I am a plant manager by profession, not a restaurant owner. I worked on the electrical system at the Gregorian University when I heard talk of improving the food service at the school. So I came up with a name and a proposal which the Rector accepted and, in 2012, we moved forward to create the *GregCafe* as a place that served the university community. Many have come to envy what we have created because the cafe is full of a sense of conviviality and community that is hard to find in other cafes in the city. The cafe is like a second home for some of our students, and it is where so many cultures cross paths; we see students and professors from all over the world come here and share their thoughts, collaborate and enjoy their time together. We manage to pick up some words in all the languages we hear in the cafe, but I like to teach a few words of Roman dialect to our customers for a good laugh and break the stress of studies.

"Everyone is welcome at *GregCafe*, even non-students, and we always have lots of visitors who like to come to our cafe.

"We never imagined that our cafe would have taken off the way it has, with a constant influx of priests, nuns, and laypeople. It has been an enormous success.

"Then last year we found these spaces in a nearby abandoned building, and we came up with the idea to create a restaurant with a high level of service and food quality; it was another challenge we took up, which resulted in what you see here now. This space was used as a storage facility, and we spent 10 months to renovate it, combining a little ancient with a bit of modern. Now, at Via dei Lucchesi 21A in Rome, we have our *Sphaeristerium Ristobar.*

"When I think of a beautiful day here in the restaurant, I think of New Year's Eve, when we had a party with our customers and all of us had fun. A bad day is when we think we did a good job, and then we find a bad review online from someone who was here, but we were unaware that they felt something was lacking. I am passionate about our work, and I am sad when this happens."

- **Francesco, what is different about this restaurant, *Sphaeristerium Ristobar?***

"This is not a tourist restaurant since we put our number one focus on quality. For example, it is challenging to find a restaurant in the center of Rome that serves fresh fish; we have a source, however, from which we obtain fresh fish every day for our restaurant. We have also been fortunate in finding our chefs, who are all young, and they create some truly unique dishes. We have created jobs for about 25 people at this restaurant, and the median age is 25. We found the perfect people to bring my idea of a restaurant into reality. We are known for our pasta dishes, but even our pastries and desserts are made here in our restaurant. We do not precook our dishes; everything is prepared to order, except for our sauces. This guarantees the freshest food when the customer orders. Pasta, meat, and all the dishes are prepared to order, so it may take 15-20 minutes to be served, but this is because we take our time to prepare each dish carefully. If you go to a restaurant and your food is served five minutes after you order it, you can be sure that it was prepared earlier or even frozen and thawed out. Our food's freshness has led to our success as a restaurant because our customers notice the difference. Every six months, we change our menu so that our customers can always find something new."

## • Why did you decide to create this type of restaurant?

"For me, the most important thing is that our clients leave fully satisfied; our customers are most important to us. We do the maximum to satisfy, and our philosophy consists of three things: quality, service, and hospitality. This work is something that I do with passion and love; I love great cooking, and I am a perfectionist. This is why the level of quality here is so high."

## • Francesco, what is your story?

"In 2006, my brother and I bought a bar for our children to work in. But then my brother died in a motorcycle accident, and the plan fell apart. Moving forward, I began my work as a plant manager at the Gregorian University, which led to my connection with, and eventual transformation of the *GregCafe*. In only three months, we renovated and completely transformed it. I put so much passion into this work, and we found a great group of young people to run the cafe. I am there from morning until evening, and I have to say that our staff is delighted. From this, we eventually founded the *Sphaeristerium Ristobar*, which took tremendous effort. The work was not only cosmetic but involved creating the kitchen, the electric and air conditioning system, and all the rest. I've learned so much in doing this work and, from being a plant manager to a restauranteur, now I have more expertise.

"As far as balancing my personal and professional life, I still have work to do in that area. The new restaurant requires my presence every day and, when the *GregCafe* is closed, the restaurant is open, and vice versa. Managing two cafes is challenging; I get up at 4:30 in the morning, and I get home around midnight. Little by little, this will get better."

- **Do you want to add anything that I didn't ask?**

"If someone wants to create something, with a group of people who share a vision and are willing to make an effort, it can be done. We have gathered a great group of people, and we are working together. We always strive to improve this restaurant, which is unique and different from all the others. I've risked everything for this restaurant, but now I am happy with the outcome.

"Before we conclude, I would like you to speak with our chefs to hear their perspective."

"My name is Fabiano."

"Mine is Cristina, and we work at *Sphaeristerium Ristobar.*"

**Cristina.** "I work at both *GregCafe* and *Sphaeristerium.* I started at the cash register, but now my responsibility covers everything, from scheduling work shifts to ordering food and supplies. If there is someone out sick or we need a hand, I always jump in. Fabiano here is our chief cook, who keeps everything going."

- **What is different about this restaurant?**

**Fabiano.** "Everything is different, beginning from the very ancient walls to the modern design and amenities, which are state of the art. The cooking fits this restaurant: maintain the Roman origins but with a modern flair. The menu changes according to the availability of fresh products. We are also always trying to improve our selection."

- **What is the philosophy here? Some restaurants use financial gain as their sole criterion. What is essential for your restaurant?**

**Fabiano.** "We are attentive to the client and provide excellent food; the client must be fully satisfied with the service, the food, and the atmosphere. We seek to provide this for each customer."

● **Can you compare your experience working here at *Sphaeristerium* and other places you have worked at?**

**Cristina.** "Where I used to work, we were only open at lunch; many celebrities would dine there because it was an expensive and well-known restaurant; journalists, actors, and others would come. But it was different; there was no relationship between the customer and myself. I brought the plate, cleared the table, then got the next customer seated. If a customer asked me what to see in Rome or where to go, I simply had no time to engage with them. I had to get that table cleared. Don't get me wrong; the food at that restaurant was great, and clients and staff were very nice, but we had to move quickly to get our customers fed, clear the table, then get the next customers seated. Here it is different; you've seen how our manager, after the customer is finished eating, comes by and offers an *amaro* or after-dinner drink with a few cookies or a sweet. People value this because they realize that they are not being rushed out, and our customers linger a bit longer because of how we treat and value them. We don't want to rush someone out; we want them to stay awhile. If they stay and enjoy their meal and linger for an hour or more, we take that as a sign that they enjoyed their experience. If someone eats quickly and rushes out, we feel like we didn't do our job well because we don't want our customers to see us as just another restaurant in Rome where you feel pushed out once you finish eating. This is what is different."

**Fabiano.** "I worked in various places, including a restaurant in London for two years, a restaurant at the airport, and several places in Rome, which all had a frenetic character: send the food out, eat, move the customer out, next! The idea that a customer could come to a place for a nice evening, a good meal with great service is such a different idea from my other work experiences. This is *Sphaeristerium*, in my view"

**Cristina.** "The cooks here are all graduates of culinary schools but are also all young and very flexible. When working with a chef who has decades of experience, it is difficult for him/her to adapt to new ideas. To modernize a traditional recipe is extremely difficult for an older chef, but our chefs do this all the time."

**Fabiano.** "Since I was a child, I loved to cook, and as I matured, this passion has stayed with me. I went to a culinary school, and I have slowly been perfecting my craft."

**Cristina.** "It was a beautiful thing when he came for the interview because he applied for the assistant position, not the main chef."

**Fabiano.** "It's true; I never pushed myself to take such a risk before. I knew Francesco, the manager, and respected his vision and experience, so it was easier to accept the challenge."

● **What is your story that led you to this point?**

**Cristina.** "I am from Ukraine, and I tried to get my degree recognized in Italy, but it wasn't possible. So I got a waitress job, and I enjoyed it; I'm a chatterbox, and I love getting to know people. I like meeting new people, and now I can use my marketing degree as my responsibilities here increase. So I am happy about this."

**Fabiano.** "I am interested in food. I've always been interested in food. Plus, it is gratifying to see a pleased customer and satisfied with what we provide."

It is difficult to measure the specter of restaurants in Rome and the vision behind each one, whether it be tourist menus, high-quality food, and service, or evangelization. Yes, there is even a restaurant in Rome that serves high-quality food as part of its higher calling.

The first time I went to *L'Eau Vive* was for my birthday when I was a student in Rome. Some friends brought me to this French-themed restaurant near the Pantheon. *L'Eau Vive* is well known in Church circles because the establishment is run by a religious order of sisters, who wear the native clothing from their various countries of origin and serve food in a fresco covered sixteenth-century palace. The decor was as impressive as the food, but it was the total experience that remained in my memory. It led me to return to the restaurant decades later after my life had dramatically changed.

Walking into *L'Eau Vive* with my partner, so long after I left the seminary, gave me the sensation of going back in time. Everything was the same yet very different. The same frescoed ceilings, the identical waitress/sisters, but the crowd was less churchy, and I was a different person. When the waitress/sister (*"wister"*?) came to take our order, she asked if we were brothers. We shook our heads. "No," I said. She was classically dressed in traditional African garb; she looked at us as if wanting more explanation. "We are friends," my partner said. She had a skeptical look on her face as if fishing for more information. I moved to change the subject, not knowing how open-minded our *wister* was regarding gay relationships. "What would you recommend tonight?" I inquired. Her face brightened as she began listing their specials. "I can also recommend a wine to complement your choices," she continued.

The *wister* then left us in peace; the food was excellent. The experience was unique: the frescoed ceilings, the quiet atmosphere, the missionary order who ran the restaurant, and the sense of history that surrounded us. I looked around and noticed that most of the other patrons were tourists with just a few tables populated by locals. When the meal was winding down, an announcement was made that the conclusion would be a short prayer service led by the sisters. Three of the women then entered our room, one with a guitar, and positioned themselves in front of the patrons; one intoned a hymn, the Ave Maria, the other strummed the guitar, and the third began doing some type of expressive dance. It seemed a bit campy to me, but it appeared to be an important moment for the sisters. I heard laughter from the table behind us, which turned out to be an Italian man and his family, who apparently felt uncomfortable with the affair. He was openly mocking the song and dance, finding it ridiculous and making sure that all of us were aware of his feelings. Observing this rude behavior, I turned and gave the sisters all of my attention and clapped at the end of their service. I sure showed him, I thought.

Rome is full of themed restaurants, which vary from medieval decor to ancient jail cell, but there was something authentic about *L'Eau Vive*; it was not trying to be something it was not. There was nothing phony; the missionary order which runs the restaurant believes in their work and tries to build relationships with people over food and drink. Women who joined this order could work at one of their restaurants in Africa, South America, the Philippines, and Europe, which opened up their horizons. When the sister who danced introduced herself as having grown up in a small village in the Andes, it seemed that this order gave their members opportunities and a sense of purpose that could be quite appealing. I was glad that we came.

Piazza Navona is the center of excitement for many visitors to Rome. It is full of street performers, student groups, cafes, and international visitors; it is a cacophony of sounds and sights. Leaving the hustle and bustle of the piazza, walking down a narrow street, one almost has to look for the Chiostro del Bramante, or Bramante Cloister, to find it. It was originally built as part of a monastery complex with the church of Santa Maria della Pace, St. Mary of Peace, next door. It is an appropriate name; a little calm oasis cut off from the city outside. Bramante designed the cloister in about 1500, and it is considered to be a masterpiece of Renaissance architecture.

The building itself is now a museum and exhibition space, but few tourists know that one can enter the building, pass the ticket counter, and go straight upstairs to their cafe. As I walked in to have my coffee in this space, I stopped in the middle of the cloister and looked up rather than immediately ascending the stairs. Visible is the coat of arms of the Renaissance Cardinal Oliviero Carafa, who commissioned the cloister. Those were the days when Cardinals were perceived as Princes of the Church; coming from wealthy families or well connected to money, they were able to create incredible examples of architecture or gather fantastic art collections. Here was his coat of arms; he must have stood in this spot, proud as he looked around at Bramante's perfectly proportioned columns with a beautiful simplicity that evoked the renewed interest in Roman and Greek architecture. Bramante was an architect of the Gothic style in Milan, but it was something completely new when he created this space. A soaring double space, with a spacious portico surrounded by arches, where I stood, and an open gallery above, where my coffee waited for me. The equilibrium and tranquility expressed the monastic flavor of many centuries ago and was still somehow encapsulated in these stones.

I ascended the stairs, placed my order, took my coffee and croissants, and headed down the corridor. I noticed seats carved in stone at the basis of the upper pillars. These were places where the monks would sit, meditate, and read. However, I wanted to be inside, so I entered the enclosed seating area with tables and comfortable chairs. I noticed a window across the dim room that opened into the church; I put my food on the table and looked over the ledge from which I could gaze at Raphael's frescoes. This seemed like a dream. I took my coffee and enjoyed its steamy smoothness as I absorbed Raphael's masterpiece.

This place is a secret in the heart of Rome; I felt conflicted about revealing it since it is a unique experience on a busy Roman day.

# Chapter 7
# Getting Lost

Nothing is more pleasurable or enlightening in Rome than setting out without a destination in mind; let feet lead and instinct be the guide. On this day, I am heading towards Piazza Navona because it "feels" right, but I am not stopping for the street entertainers; I go behind the piazza and find Via dei Coronari, a beautiful, mostly walking street lined with shops and cafes. Making my way towards the Vatican, I stop to look in these overpriced stores filled with unique antiques, including paintings, busts of Roman emperors, and various well crafted beautiful objects that serve no practical purpose. The common denominator that I notice in all of these shops is that they all lack customers. "How do they pay their rent?" I wonder out loud. "How do they pay their mortgage, buy groceries, or make car payments?" I continue to say to nobody in particular. Year after year, decade after decade, I have seen these beautiful shops along this fascinating street, always without customers. Perhaps they come late at night, I wonder.

My feet tell me to head back towards Piazza Farnese, so I cross the Corso and take a back street exiting in front of the French Embassy in the piazza; on the corner is a church, doors wide open, which I enter. Two nuns are sitting in the back of the church with these weird straps over their veil that makes it look like they are wearing a helmet. Later that night, I looked up what that odd headgear was all about and learned that it represents Christ's crown of thorns. They are called Bridgettine nuns and were founded in 1344; they run a little known guesthouse on that spot. Once I stopped staring at the nuns' heads, I sat down to enjoy the peace. The church was amazingly clean, classic baroque, with a lightness about it that lifted my spirit. I said a prayer of gratitude, took one last glance at the helmeted nuns, then left.

My instinct took over and urged me on to the Jewish Quarter, a light-filled area with great food but with a sad history. The Jewish population was swept up in the Reformation and Counter-Reformation religious tides when Pope Paul IV moved Rome's Jews into a flood-prone area of seven acres in 1555. The Jewish inhabitants lived within these walls for three centuries, having to obey a curfew and employment restrictions until the Ghetto's walls were torn down in 1848. The Jewish residents were then granted full rights and citizenship during this period and enjoyed this boost in freedom until World War II. When the Nazis occupied Rome, they demanded that the Jewish community pay 50 kilograms of gold as a ransom or face immediate deportation. Chief Rabbi Israel Zolli went to the Vatican for help and obtained a loan for the full amount, which would be paid back after the war. But the loan was not needed since so many, Jews and non-Jews, stepped forward to donate their gold watches and jewelry to help with the ransom. But the gold payment only delayed the arrest and deportation of about 2,000 Jews, half of whom were sent to Auschwitz. Few survived; only 16 returned to Rome.

As I make my way through the Jewish Quarter, I stop to see the commemorative stone plaque to the victims of the Nazi extermination of October 16, 1943. I then turn down a side street where, among the cobblestones in front of the houses, are the names engraved in bronze of those who were forcibly removed and sent to concentration camps that day. I pause and look down to read the bronze cobblestone at my feet: "Here lived Silvia Sermoneta, born 1897, arrested on October 10, 1943, deported, Auschwitz, assassinated July 15, 1944, on Via Salaria." I move on down the street to read: "Here lived Costanza Sonnino, born 1909, arrested on October 4, 1943, deported, Auschwitz, died in an unknown place at an unknown time." The festive restaurant and shop filled streets are a dramatic contrast to the tragedy that unfolded in October of 1943, and as I wander through those side streets, I find myself caught up in the fear and tragedy of that day.

As I step out onto the main road in that neighborhood, the Via del Portico d'Ottavia, my feet direct me to a more lighthearted monument. Soon, I find myself in front of the Fountain of the Turtles, built during the sixteenth century. It's a beautiful little plaza where the fountain lies outside of a building with a bricked-up window. The water is gurgling, the sun is shining, and there are few tourists here. Like all historical places in Rome, this also has its story. It is one of love and endurance, as Duke Muzio Mattei had the fountain built overnight, outside of the window where his beloved was staying, to win this woman's heart and the approval of her father. Permission given, the marriage took place, and so that no one else would be able to view that fountain from that angle, the window was bricked up—the crazy things one does for love.

It's time to leave this area, and I feel pulled towards the Forum, so I set out in that direction by foot, eventually arriving in Piazza Venezia, where the "wedding cake" building draws tourists for photos, but I am indifferent to it. I walk past, cross the street, and find myself in Trajan's Market, the oldest shopping complex in ancient Rome, dating from 113 CE. There were over 150 shops and offices, offering goods from all over the Empire, including fruits and vegetables, spices, and fast food. This is a less-visited section of the Forum, and it is great to be away from the crowds. Still, the sun is beating down, and I am ready for another adventure, so I circle the back of Trajan's Market and make my way to the Angelicum. At this university, I obtained my degrees in philosophy and theology.

It had been decades since I was here last, and I didn't even know if I could gain access since I wasn't a student. But I climb those same stairs that I went up and down when I was 19 and soon find myself in the courtyard, surrounded by classrooms, where I had spent the academic period of my youth. There were few people around, so I explore and go back to where the bar was; it is still there but closed today. I walk past an African man with a Roman collar who looks me up and down as if he wanted to eat me alive. I continue walking through the corridors until I find myself in the garden area. Memories of taking a philosophy exam with an Italian professor flood my mind. We paced up and down the garden paths; he asked me open-ended questions about metaphysical subjects, and I answered as best I could at the time. It was a warm and sunny memory, though probably nerve-racking back then. Returning to the courtyard once again, I try one of the classroom doors, which is unlocked! So I search for and find the classroom where I took my philosophy classes the first year I was in Rome; I open the door and sit down at the desk where I had sat so many years before.

Here I felt I was part of a great history; the Angelicum has its roots in 1580 as the College of St. Thomas and then becoming a full-fledged Pontifical University in 1906. Since 1932 the campus had been located on this spot which was laid out more like a monastery, having served that purpose before the Angelicum moved in and through whose corridors illustrious alumni such as Pope John Paul II made their way to class. I sit here, reflecting on my memories and the wave of history that reached until this present moment. I feel baffled by it all but also grateful.

Somehow my feet had led me full circle; I was back where I began my education in Rome reflecting on how my life had unfolded in ways that I would have never believed had a Roman fortune-teller foresaw it all. It was in this place that my love for this city had sprouted; from here I took secret excursions to explore the churches and monuments, from here I took the archeology classes that gave rise to my fascination with Rome underground; it was in this place that Rome began to seduce me and to this place she brought me this day.

In an afternoon I had left contemporary Rome, found myself among nuns from an order dating from the 1300s, was surrounded by the Holocaust, swept up by a fountain of love, walked back in time to a mall built in 113 CE and ended up at a university founded in the 1500s where I began my higher education. Only Rome can offer so much.

# Chapter 8
# According to Romans

Who is a Roman, and how do they define their identity? What do Romans think of their city? What do they feel about the history, the buildings, the tourists, the streets, and the culture? I asked some of these "true Romans" to share their story.

"My name is Lilli, and I was born in Rome and have lived here all my life, but I have also traveled extensively, especially in the United States."

"My name is Sergio, and, though my family is from Milan, I have lived in Rome since I was 5 years old and so consider myself to be a Roman."

"My name is Lorenzo, and I am 29 years old; I was born and raised in Rome but I have also lived and worked in London and Berlin."

"My name is Carmela, and I was born and grew up in Rome, moved to the United States when I was in my twenties; I lived there for twenty-five years and then moved back to Rome, where I live now."

- **Tell me about your life in Rome?**

**Lilli.** "I am 53 years old, and I've always lived in Rome; my mother still lives in the same house where I grew up.

My childhood was serene; I was born in the 1960s during an economic boom in Italy, and this was a time when many Italians had larger families. But then in the 1970s, there was a financial crisis; in Rome, you were permitted to only drive your car every other day because of the lack of gasoline. The 1970s were combative years, years of activism, and political struggles over abortion, divorce, the right to work, etc.

"Both of my parents were working professionals when I was a child. Rome was more livable during that time. The city has changed so much. When I was a child, the streets were our playground; our house was on a road where few cars passed, and we played all day with other children; the streets were safe back then. This type of life doesn't exist in Rome anymore. It's no longer possible for our children to play on the streets; it's no longer safe.

"I have sweet memories of Rome as a beautiful place, but I cannot say this is true today."

**Sergio.** "I was born in Milan, but I have lived in Rome since I was 5 years old. We lived in the northern part of the city where I attended school; when I was young, I thought Rome was just the neighborhood where I lived. I have come to appreciate the city as an adult, and I often ride my motorcycle to other towns, but none compares with Rome.

"I work in Milan periodically, and I sometimes compare the mentalities of the two places. Rome is full of a historical culture preserved for thousands of years in the buildings and monuments, whereas in Milan, the buildings express that things change quickly. My work is in computer science, and I am often in contact with many different cultures; in Rome, we have the mentality of helping one another to create something greater. A gift of the work environment here is that it is second nature to help and support one another; the culture of Milan is more individualistic as each one focuses on the challenges of his/her own life."

**Carmela.** "I was born in Rome in 1962, and I lived here until I was 27; then I moved to the US and returned to Rome in 2014.

"I have a mother and two sisters, and we always lived in the same house in the same neighborhood; I went to the university in Rome, where I studied classics, which includes art history and architecture. Then I moved to the States; I was a follower. I followed my husband to Berkley, then Louisiana, and then my last city was Minneapolis. After this, I returned to Rome.

"So my life is divided into two parts; it was like having two homes: before the US and afterward.

"I lived in Prati[16]; I was able to walk pretty much everywhere, and, in my teenage years, while wandering around, I could always discover something new, or I would find something that would become mine. I remember walking along the Tiber, having this feeling while strolling under these trees, ever-changing, that these are somehow my trees and my river. I can remember returning to my home, even after years, seeing the city lights from my window; this gave me a beautiful feeling of being back home.

"When I studied art history and architecture, the ancient buildings in Rome became alive. You fall in love with some things in Rome. Like going into the French church and seeing that Caravaggio painting, you fall in love with it, and it becomes yours. Perhaps it is comparable to other cities, but Rome remains pretty much the same, unlike other places. The people change, some of the businesses change, but the city remains identical.

"The beauty of Rome is that it has so many hidden narrow little streets, so you walk in Trastevere, and then you come across something you've never seen before. You

---

16 Prati is the area of Rome north of the Vatican, known for its elegant buildings, great restaurants and large avenues, some say it resembles a Parisian neighborhood.

come upon a church that people come to visit, and, at a certain point, it becomes yours. It becomes different when it becomes yours.

"I returned to Rome for my family, not for the city. I needed help in my life, and I needed my family's support. In the back of my mind, there was this feeling that I was returning home. Though I came back for the people, at the same time, I found my city again. I teach Latin and Greek in a high school in my neighborhood, which I enjoy very much. I have the same background as many of my students because we live in the same area, so we feel connected.

"The city is more than monuments; it is a fabric that you are part of.

"We do have this strong sense of family; my sisters are here; my mother is here. We don't move around, so this makes the city and family life harmonious.

"In the beginning, it wasn't easy since I had to go back to work, but slowly I got involved with my job. I had one child here with me, and slowly I regained my relationship with the city."

### • What do you love about Rome? What do you hate?

**Lilli.** "Rome is incredible for many reasons: the climate, the history, the parks, the architecture, the alleys, the surprises. I like Rome because I was born here; I like Rome because all of my affections are here. But I don't like that Rome is mistreated; it has been abandoned by those who should be taking care of it. There is a lot of rudeness; a sense of citizenship is missing. I see the difference when I travel; when I go north or to the United States, there is more care for the cities than in Rome. It is a place that has many challenges, including the difficulty of just building a subway; every time they dig a tunnel, they find another hidden building or monument.

"The strange thing about Rome that makes me feel bad

is that we value cleanliness and order inside the house, but outside in public spaces, it's chaos. We don't seem to have the mentality to take care of our streets and our public spaces, and this always makes me feel bad."

**Sergio.** "What I don't like about Rome is a certain mentality in which people throw their garbage on the ground, where parents teach their children to "fare il furbo": to be dishonest to try to get ahead. What I love about it is the climate and having the beach nearby where I love to go in the spring and summer."

**Lorenzo.** "I love and hate the almost complete freedom and chaos, familiarity, and corruption, historic beauty, and the coldness that is typical of Rome."

**Carmela.** "The US spoiled me in some ways. For example, I can't accomplish anything here over the phone; I have to go to the place of business in person. The city is dirty and is more crowded than it used to be. There are few resources. More immigrants need a good job. But I see them as an asset to the city. Immigrants are the only ones who clean the city. There is this guy who cleans the sidewalk on my street, and you can give him a few coins if you want. If you leave a chair outside, it will be gone the next day; he takes care of the street. These people fill a need that the city doesn't.

"You can see problems everywhere together with beauty. The busses are not perfect like in Berlin; here, maybe they are late because the bus driver is engaged in an argument about soccer!

"Those 25 years in the States are part of my life, but they didn't change my relationship with Rome. Six years after returning, I go to work every day. I see my family when I can, and I am back in my routine. But because of limited free time, I only find myself walking through the city when I show an American friend around.

"There is magic in Rome, but tourists see only a part of the city; they come for a short time, and they don't have to deal with the bureaucracy. When you see the sunset over the Tiber, it is magical. If you love history, imagining ancient Romans walking around the Forum, it is magical. But the Romans working in their shops from 7 in the morning until 7 at night sometimes don't see the magic, yet they know the ancient buildings and history and art and culture are there; it is comforting somehow.

"If I think about my mother, who used to have a store where she worked long hours, she did experience the magic; maybe on a Sunday, she would walk around the historical center, always aware that she was part of this almost eternal city. Even without intentionally going to see the sites, you can still experience that feeling; you know there is one church or one street or one monument that has been there for a long time, which gives you a window into that magic."

### • How do Romans feel about tourists?

**Lilli.** "This is one thing that I have reflected on more than once: we are used to seeing the things in Rome, whereas the people who are standing there taking selfies in Piazza Venezia are happy and enthusiastic; this makes me look at that monument differently. It stupefies me, like the ruins all over Rome that I don't even notice anymore, which the tourists gather around and marvel over, it makes me ask myself, 'maybe it's worth it to come to Rome to see these things.' This makes an impact on me."

**Lorenzo.** "Toward strangers, we Romans tend to be both arrogant and friendly in a bizarre way. Prejudices are huge, but often in an amusing way. Poor African migrants and North American spoilt Ivy League students chilling at FAO or John Cabot's University are looked down upon from the very same pulpit of grounded ignorance, but - as I said - in a quite caricatural, funny, and at the same time 'Roman' way. We make fun of, judge, and admire, all at the same moment."

### • What do you feel about the church?

**Lilli.** "First and foremost, I am a believer. In Rome, given the Vatican's presence, many religious groups travel here. As far as my relationship with the church, it has evolved a lot. I don't believe in judging anyone, neither the Pope nor anyone else. I live the church in my relationship with God, and I avoid all the polemics around Pope Francis.

"There is one thing I want to say: Pope Francis is all for immigrants, and he asks to open our doors and hearts to refugees, and he is right in saying that. But for many of us, either living in poverty or barely getting by, so many immigrants end up increasing poverty. The Pope keeps saying: 'Open your doors, open your doors,' well, you open your doors then!

"A few years ago, the Vatican took in a group of about 30 immigrants and housed them, but then some of them fled because they didn't want to follow the rules. These poor people escape poverty and violence by coming here to Rome, then they flee the housing offered to them? Some rules have to be accepted; it's not that we don't want immigrants, but we want immigrants to accept the fact that there are laws that we all have to follow.

"Everyone has their right to worship, and I have no issue with this, but sometimes I wonder if Christianity will disappear from our culture."

**Sergio.** "I have a good faith relationship and attend Mass almost every Sunday; my children also attend Catholic schools, and my relationship with the church has always been positive. I don't think priests or nuns are better or worse than other people; they are simply people that have made this choice. I see many contributions that the church makes here, especially schools for our children."

**Lorenzo.** "The church can tell you a lot about Rome's soul: a huge, ridiculously rich and self-confident facade which hides mostly very weak and spiritually poor human beings. The church is the main employer and political power in the city, actively lobbying on almost every aspect of socio-economic life. But it is also an organization full of good and strong people, really fighting and struggling for peace on earth, but the closer you get to the physical buildings of St. Peter's or the Lateran, the less you'll find these good people. I've had several young and passionate priests as friends who almost gave up. That said, I believe that the church was pretty much born as a mostly political institution, trying to bring together all deeply different cultural expressions of the city through its tumultuous history with an often extremely pragmatic spirit."

**Carmela.** "My feelings about the church are part of a long history. I grew up in a parish (*oratorio*); my mother was working, and so my sister and I spent our afternoons at the parish grounds where we played soccer and other sports. Then when I was about 14, in high school, I left the activities at the parish. I started my university studies and found another type of experience in the movement, Communion and Liberation, which helped me in my life. It was a different way to live the church's life in the university, meaning that I found companions in life. This became a more adult relationship with the church, a more beautiful relationship than before. I met many faces, and my life is made of these many faces, and some of them showed me that Christ could become a companion in my life. When Christ became a companion through a person, things changed for me.

"I have had many difficult circumstances in my life, especially after I separated from my husband with my four children; without those companions, it would have been more challenging to leave that situation that I needed to leave. When your hope relies on someone who then disappears for some reason, life becomes precarious. Then someone shows you that your hope doesn't consist of a single person; this gives you a different perspective and the desire to start again. This is a beautiful thing. For me, life gave me this, and it was vital for me to have these people in my life.

"For me, the church is experiencing something in the present; if it were just putting something into practice that happened in the past, I wouldn't do that; I would get bored after five minutes. Living the church with people that have the same desire as you is very different. This is what the church is for me."

### • What is most important to you?

**Lilli.** "Love is essential to me, not only towards my husband and children but as a fundamental value. What is also most important to me is that I am trying to open my mind and have begun asking myself this question: why am I here? What difference does my life make?

"The fact that I've had the beautiful experience of becoming a mother has opened up the horizons of my life, which I never imagined.

"One thing I can say is that life is surprising; I would have never imagined how things would unfold. Today I try to give meaning to that which I do."

**Carmela.** "As a mother, it is important that my children be happy, especially because I have a daughter who is having a difficult time. But beyond this, it is important to reach happiness with a capital "H." I will say that I have some moments that I experience this and some moments less. Still, I am lucky enough to be able to say that I am sometimes happy in that sense, full of gratitude and joy for that single instant of my life that can be repeated again and again. What I mean by that happiness with a capital "H" is that I was given a life, one life, my life, and that's what I need, to live my life because it is mine, not someone else's, and to be happy with the life I was given.

"That is what is most important for me now that I am 57, and I have lived a good part of my life. If I look back, I don't have any regrets since I am happy that this is the life I was given. Even to the point that I can see my ex-husband and be happy, rather than seeing someone who hurt me, I see him, with all his defects, as a person."

### ● How do Romans feel about rules and laws?

**Sergio.** "An example of this: in Rome, if I go through a red light and there is no police officer, there is no consequence. In the US, if I go through a red light, I get a ticket. In Italy, there is a difference between doing something against the law or another person. I think respect for the law is a good thing, but here in Italy, it is more fluid. This is not always positive; if a bar offers free coffees to the local police officers, the police won't give a fine to cars parked illegally in front of that business. There is particular favoritism that works against the common good. "

**Lorenzo.** "Romans are often fatalists that don't expect to get any effective help from any institution, but at the same time, they take everything they do get for granted. The monuments and ruins are seen as everyone's personal property and therefore nobody's property. There is a sort of endemic decadent atmosphere to the whole city, which makes it natural to keep on destroying it and impossible to take anything seriously from an institutional point of view."

**Carmela.** "Laws are not respected here in the way they are in the US; not only traffic laws but in all areas. Here someone may not file taxes for years and years, and nobody realizes it. It is so strange. The government keeps promising to fix this system, but it will never happen.

"Also, in the US, records are kept on everything; you go through a red light or commit some transgression, and it's on your permanent record. Here in Rome, there are no records; you can go to a job interview, and nobody will ask you for a background check. You always start brand new. In this society, you don't feel punished forever. In the United States, I've seen teenagers do something unwise, and it could follow them around for the rest of their lives. In Italy, we don't have this idea of a permanent record; it is a more forgiving society. They will look at you for what you are and not your credit score or past transgressions."

### • How do Romans feel about friendship and family?

**Lorenzo.** "As in most of Italy, friends and family often tend to meld together in one concept and reality: loyalty is its main feature. On the other hand — for both men and women — being real friends and family includes making fun of each other: "mettere un amico in mezzo"; this means "putting a friend in the middle" of social discomfort or embarrassment to let him somehow grow and realize how he is. Kissing on the cheeks and hugging are common between both sexes. Family is similar to the experience of friendship: Roman men love to look macho outside and hug their mums at home!"

**Carmela.** "I can only speak from my experience. Friendship is precious in Italy as a general concept. I returned to Rome for the people, for my family and friends, because they make such a difference in my life. I only took one of my children with me since the others were older and didn't want to come. It was a huge decision, but I came back because I needed my family and friends. I had friends in the US, and I know that you can have real friendships everywhere, no matter which society you are in. But the concept of friendship is more robust in Italy and the idea of family; we don't leave home until 25 or 26, we try to live near our other family members. The US is more of a mobile society.

"Friendship is like second nature for us; I think it is the same for Americans, but the US culture is based on the idea that you can do whatever you want, that you can be your own person, that you can succeed on your own; for an Italian, we don't want to be on our own, but we want to share our life with others. We don't desire to build our fortune and future as it is instilled in American culture. I can see this mindset in my American kids; since kindergarten, they are taught that they can do everything by themselves. American students don't cheat, but they don't help each other in school either because if I help her, she may do better than me. I am a teacher, and I see a different approach in our schools. Unfortunately, my students do cheat, but cheating only brings you to a certain point; in the end, you have to know the material. But our students want to help each other; this is an example of the difference in mentalities. In the US, you have to think about yourself first and then the others if you want to be your best. In Italy, it is the opposite; my students help each other any way they can. The mentality is to help each other out; of course, some students are more competitive, but competition is not a value, and ambition is not a value. In Italian, the word 'ambizione' is something negative; it is someone who will step on others to get what he/she wants. So the word "ambition" is negative, and this was hard for me when I was learning English because it was used as a positive trait when referring to people to be admired.

"Family is the same thing; we have this sense of 'extended family' or *famiglia allargata*. Here it is very typical that your sister or mother takes care of your kids while you are at work; it is second nature to help each other out. Yesterday, for example, on the day of the Epiphany, I went to my sister's for lunch, and there were my siblings and 11 kids, and it is natural for us to gather on that holiday. This is what I would like for my children; when they are here, they experience this, but upon returning to the US they barely talk. When they are in Rome, they bond and feel connected, which is lost when they return to the US."

### • How do you think Romans and Americans are the most different? How are they the same?

**Lilli.** "I believe that we Italians, and Romans in particular, are finicky towards things and wary when it comes to people. But once we have welcomed someone into our lives, we are very affectionate and loyal. There is a saying: 'Always add a plate at the table for an extra friend.' There is always room for a friend.

"I have to admit also that we Romans like it when someone takes notice of us."

**Carmela.** "Americans and Romans are similar because every person, at the core, is the same. The environment plays some role, but, in essence, they are alike.

"What I was saying about Romans or Italians is that, somehow, this core or heart is under layers, whether it be job, money, anything, that core can almost disappear under all those layers. In Italy, maybe we have fewer layers, and so it's easier to see that core and uncover it.

"Our lives make us a little different, but we are the same in the end. We cover our hearts with layers, sometimes to move forward because it is hard, but I think an Italian can uncover this core easier than many Americans."

### • How are Romans different from other Italians?

**Lilli.** "I believe that Romans, compared with Italians from other areas, are more open to what is diverse. We are used to living with foreigners in our midst for thousands of years, and we have a strong ability to adapt. We are less rigid and so are more able to solve problems. Romans are pragmatic people."

**Sergio.** "Your typical Roman is open-minded, friendly, and values hospitality. The negative aspect is this idea of being 'sly' (*furbo*) to get around the law, get around paying taxes and get around being ethical. But this is also a part of the mentality of some Italians and not just of Romans. You are never treated as a foreigner in Rome; I think this comes from thousands of years of influx of people. You could go to another Italian city or town and feel like an outsider, but this doesn't happen in Rome. You are embraced for who you are.

"In the North people tend to be better organized but they are also not as warm-hearted as people in Rome and southern Italy. Perhaps this is because of historical reasons in which parts of Italy were occupied and dominated by foreign powers and so may feel influenced by French or Austrian culture whereas southern Italy is a different world. Italy has never become as united as, for example, Germany did after the Cold War. Each area was dominated and influenced by different cultural forces and this adds to the idea of 'two Italys', north and south. Perhaps this is our weakness but it is also our strength since this has added to the richness of our culture."

● **What is your favorite place in Rome? Why?**

**Lorenzo.** "Climbing over the fence and up the Palatine Hill at night and looking down on the illuminated Forum from the Capitoline Hill with a good bottle of wine and a good friend is my perfect way to enjoy the city."

**Carmela.** "I have a favorite place in Rome; I like Piazza Farnese because, every morning, I researched for my dissertation in the beautiful library inside Palazzo Farnese. My dissertation was about the Etruscans, and I went to that library for months. This holds a special place in my heart."

**Sergio.** "The place I like most in Rome is not the city but the beach. I love riding my motorcycle to the sea, which, being in Ostia, is still Rome in the 'enlarged' sense of the word. The open spaces, the water, the sun, and the sea are my favorite part of Rome. Sometimes I have so much on my mind from work, but it all vanishes when I go to the beach. I feel at peace in a way that is hard to explain. Yes, I can go to the historical center and have an excellent time, but that is not my preference. Not the city, but the sea is where I want to be in Rome."

### • What do you do in your free time?

**Lilli.** "With a family, I don't have a lot of free time, but when I do, I play sports and spend time with friends; I especially enjoy having friends over for dinner. When we are tired from our workweek, we often watch movies on Netflix on weekends."

**Sergio.** "I love working in my garden; I find this very peaceful. But I don't have much free time; when I get home, I often have to keep working in the evenings and on Saturdays. But I also love going to the beach when I can escape."

**Lorenzo.** "I love biking and roller skating through the city's chaotic streets and showing the many angry cab drivers that there are better and more fun ways to get around. I love to understand things, but I prefer talking and listening rather than reading."

### • What is your favorite activity in Rome?

**Lilli.** "My favorite activity is taking care of my family; this is my passion and gives meaning to everything else. Sometimes this is fatiguing, but it is also rewarding.

"Getting together with friends can be challenging;

unfortunately, I've had to give up the spontaneity with which I lived. It is difficult just to let oneself go; it is as if we wear different masks to survive in what sometimes feels like a desert."

**Carmela.** "I love to walk and wander around. Whenever I have the time, I do this because it is beautiful, and it gives me time to think amid these beautiful buildings. My second favorite activity is to go shopping with my girls."

● **If you could describe Rome in three words, what would they be?**

**Lilli.** "Unique, contradictory, supportive."

**Sergio.** "Eternal City: the only city where the culture extends back so far and yet is so present today. Dirty: it is a filthy eternal city. I used more than three words, I know. I will sum it up: eternal, city, dirty."

**Lorenzo.** "Beautiful, dirty, and mysterious."

**Carmela.** "Beautiful. Old (not only age but life that has been here so long). Meaningful."

● **Is there anything else you would like to add?**

**Carmela.** "I have so much affection for what I do every day: in 7 minutes I can get to work; I teach in a beautiful school by the river, I see the trees, the Tiber and the ancient buildings from my window. I have to say that I love my daily life, my neighborhood and I enjoy doing these things every day."

# Chapter 9
# Underground Rome: The Golden House of Nero and the Houses of Livia and Augustus

*In no other matter did he act more wasteful than in building a house that stretched from the Palatine to the Esquiline Hill, which he originally named "Transitoria" [House of Passages], but when soon afterward it was destroyed by fire and rebuilt he called it "Aurea" [Golden House]. A house whose size and elegance these details should be sufficient to relate: Its courtyard was so large that a 120-foot colossal statue of the Emperor himself stood there; it was so spacious that it had a mile-long triple portico; also there was a pool of water like a sea, that was surrounded by buildings which gave it the appearance of cities; and besides that, various rural tracts of land with vineyards, cornfields, pastures, and forests, teeming with every kind of animal both wild and domesticated. In other parts of the house, everything was covered in gold and adorned with jewels and mother-of-pearl; dining rooms with fretted ceilings whose ivory panels could be turned so that flowers or perfumes from pipes were sprinkled down from above; the main hall of the dining rooms was round, and it would turn constantly day and night like the Heavens; there were baths, flowing with seawater and with the sulfur springs of the Albula; when he dedicated this house, that had been completed in this manner, he approved of it only so much as to say that he could finally begin to live like a human being.* (Suetonius, The Lives of the Caesars).[17]

---

17 Suetonius, The Twelve Caesars, trans. Robert Graves, ed. James Rives (London: Penguin, 2007).

Ahhh, the Golden House of Nero, where ego meets architecture! I was ready for an underground adventure and made my way over to the *Domus Aurea*, Nero's Golden House, facing the coliseum. Since I had no ticket, I would roll the dice and see if I could get in.

I made my way up the hill towards the red brick structure; I asked about getting in at the ticket counter. "English is sold out," the lady at the window responded to my question in Italian. "But there is space on the Italian tour which begins in 15 minutes," she said. "Fantastico!" I said. "Un biglietto." One ticket.

A few minutes later, I was donning my yellow hard-hat and listening to the archeologist's introduction. She explained that the Domus Aurea's discovery occurred in the late fifteenth century when a young Roman fell into a hole, looked up, and found himself inside Nero's Golden House. Many followed after him, gazing at the frescoed and stuccoed vaults and gaining inspiration that influenced Renaissance art. But they only saw the ceilings because the house had been filled with rubble, supporting arches were installed in it, and Trajan's baths had been built on top. It was as if there was a deliberate attempt to wipe out all memories of Nero and his house, yet here we were inside!

The layout of the Domus Aurea had been altered due to the supporting structures for the baths. The tops of some rooms had been sliced off to create an even surface above, so the archeologist showed us a diagram to explain that we were entering the house through a tunnel built in Trajan's time and not through the main entrance. She then encouraged us to follow her inside and to go back in time to the dwelling of that ruthless and fascinating Emperor.

Though he was not in Rome during the Great Fire of 64 AD, many blamed Nero for the conflagration. It was no secret that Nero wanted to build a palace on the Oppian Hill but could not get the Senate's permission since it was already covered with residential and commercial buildings. Once the fire cleared out the area, Nero initiated construction almost immediately, leaving many Romans to suspect his involvement.

As we made our way through the dark corridor and entered the house, I asked myself, "Why?" Why build a home that covered over 200 acres, decorated with the best artwork looted from the ancient world, with an artificial lake, woods, and a selfie statue that towered 120 feet? Then to live in the unfinished house only a few years before committing suicide in 68 AD? What gives, Nero?

Some imagination is needed when visiting the Golden House today because most frescoes are faded, the marble has been removed, the layout has been altered, and the windows and open spaces have been bricked over. But something of the beauty of the place remains, and that is what is so perplexing. If Nero was a complete lunatic, how could he have supervised the construction of such a magnificent place? He had both his mother killed and his first wife, and then he kicked his second wife to death. Nero also liked to throw garden parties using human torches to illuminate the festivities. If Nero was evil and insane, he apparently either had some moments of sanity or simply knew how to supervise the construction despite his madness.

As we made our way through some of the 140 rooms thus far discovered, the decor reveals specific patterns, bringing to life the legends and myths of mostly Greek origin, telling the stories of heroes and gods from the past. Scenes from the Trojan War appear again and again since Nero, and the Romans, liked to think of themselves as descendants from the Trojan royal line, and Nero himself saw Aeneas as his great great great great great great great grandfather! Whether based in history or wishful thinking, the Roman link to the Trojan War was alluded to in many rooms where Nero would have passed the time.

When we came into the room shaped like an octagon, with an oculus in the middle of the ceiling. The archeologist told us the story of another octagonal room in Nero's house, not yet discovered, which had a revolving coffered ceiling under which guests feasted while being misted with rose water and showered with flower petals. But the price to be paid for dining there with

Nero could include handing over one's wife if Nero took a liking to her; the husband had to continue to pretend to enjoy the festivities as his spouse, and the Emperor had sexual relations in the adjoining room. It is difficult to imagine guests clamoring to get an invitation to Nero's table.

There were the remains of an interior waterfall in the room in which we stood, lending to the feeling of peace and tranquility that must have permeated that space when it was empty. Yet when Nero and his guests were present, the serenity of rippling water would have been in contrast to the discomfort of not knowing just what this Emperor might do at any given moment. Nero could have been standing where I was, looking over the wife of one of his senators. He could have been discussing his concert the night before, during which he was known to sing and perform for so many hours that women would feign childbirth just to get out. Or I may be standing where this woman stood, hoping beyond hope that the Emperor would not take a liking to her and feeling powerless in that situation. The waterfall, the light from the oculus, the beauty, the fear, the degradation, the insanity, the political maneuvering, the plotting, the longing to leave, and the absurdity of the situation in this space where I stood.

As we continued making our way through the Domus Aurea, I thought it curious that, in the effort to destroy Nero's memory and bury his house, it was preserved to a great extent better than any other emperor's dwelling in Rome. Room after room, fresco after fresco spoke of this man's obsession with his lineage, with power and impressing the world with the biggest, the best, and the unattainable.

In June of the year 68 CE, Nero realized how precarious his position had become: first, the Praetorian guards abandoned allegiance to the Emperor. Then, the legions in Germany began to support a rival emperor. Once he realized his life was in danger, Nero attempted to flee; he went to Ostia to try to take a ship to safety, but the officers would not obey his orders. Nero then hatched a plan to go to Parthia and ask for protection. Abandoning this idea, he sat down to write a speech to beg for the forgiveness and protection of the people of Rome; he planned to ask that he be sent to Egypt to rule the province. But he never gave that speech (which was found later) since he realized that he might be torn to pieces on his way to the Forum. So Nero decided to return to his Golden House, and he fell asleep.

It was almost midnight on June 8, 68 CE, when, feeling that something was wrong, Nero awoke. Getting up from his bed, he found that the palace guard was gone. He sent messages to his friends staying at the palace but received no responses; going to their rooms, he found them empty. He began going from room to room, crying out, "Have I neither friend nor foe?" Some freedmen appeared, still loyal to Nero; they helped him disguise himself and flee Rome to take refuge in a freedman's villa a few miles outside the city.

The Senate, meanwhile, was in a predicament. Nero was the last of the Julio-Claudian line; his death would mean that the deified dynasty would end. The Senate debated how to preserve Nero's life while curbing his insanity and decided to send for the Emperor to appear at the Senate where some type of deal could be worked out.

Nero, meanwhile, received a false message that the Senate had ordered his execution; he believed they were coming to take him to the Forum to execute him. He would never submit to this, but he also could not bring himself to commit suicide. "Kill yourself first to give me courage!" he ordered one of his companions, as horses' hooves sounded outside. "What an artist dies in me," Nero kept muttering. Grabbing the sword, Nero still couldn't plunge it into his chest, so he asked his secretary to do the deed.

When the horsemen entered and saw Nero was dying, they tried to stop the bleeding, not for any love for him but to preserve his dynasty, but to no avail. Nero died on June 9, 68 CE, and was buried in the area of Santa Maria del Popolo in the Piazza del Popolo.

I had my fill of Nero as our tour guide led us into the sunlight; it was a fantastic visit, but I was ready for some sanity. I headed over to the Palatine Hill.

It was around 770 BCE when Romulus and Remus were born, the twins at the center of Rome's founding. The legend has it that, to spare their lives, their mother Princess Rhea Silvia put them in a basket in the Tiber; when a wolf found them, they were nursed rather than eaten; they then grew up under the care of the shepherd Faustulus. Reaching manhood, the two fought over the significance of signs and the founding of a new city; Romulus killed his brother Remus and so Rome was born.

Augustus knew this story well and utilized it to raise the prestige of his reign as Emperor by building his palace next to that spot where that basket was found.

I was not happy about standing in a long line to get my tickets to enter the Forum and the Palatine, but it was my fault for not planning. I debated whether to return another day but then told myself to chill out and relax. Forty minutes later, I was inside.

Walking across the Palatine area, where there is not much more than low exposed walls and fragments, can be a letdown, but I had my ticket, with time stamp, to get inside the houses of Augustus and Livia; I was excited. "Dove stanno le case di Augusto e Livia? - Where are the houses of Augustus and Livia?" I asked the guard, finding no signs pointing the way. After getting some complicated directions, I decided to follow some other tourists who seemed like they knew where they were going. "Eccolo!" I said, turning a corner.

I had no idea about what I was about to see, and when the small group of us English speakers stepped inside the house of Livia, I couldn't stop myself from blurting out: "Wow!"

I stood in a rectangular atrium, which was open on one side facing three large fresco covered adjoining rooms. As I gazed into the first room, I noticed winged human figures almost like angels, but without the plump faces, along with decorations painted to look like marble inlay and details suggesting a garden. But then the recorded narration began, and a surprisingly well-crafted presentation started, which was able to give an idea, through projections, of what the rooms looked like during Livia's lifetime.

We moved to the central room where there is a faded fresco, which the narrator explained was a depiction of the cyclops Polyphemus and the sea nymph Galatea. It was interesting that Livia chose this image as the center of her house because it was the story of unrequited love: Polyphemus, an oversized, bitter one-eyed almost monster, fell in love with the lovely Galatea. She was not interested in Polyphemus because of who he was, and also, her heart was given to another, a certain shepherd named Acis, son of Pan. But Polyphemus never gave up, spending day after day scanning the sea looking for Galatea. The cyclops then came up with a plan: he would make a set of pipes and play them to lure Galatea while calling out her name, but she ignored his playing and instead chose to hide with her love, Acis. At a certain point, Polyphemus discovered the couple and flew into a fury; Galatea dove into the sea while Acis took off running on land. Polyphemus grabbed a piece of the mountain and hurled it at Acis, who was struck and buried by it, his blood oozing out of the rocks. Galatea saw the whole thing and cried out to the gods to sanctify that spot. At that instant, a stream of water shot up and quickly became the river which flows from Aetna to the sea; it became the testimony of the love between Acis and Galatea.

Did this story have anything to do with the relationship between Livia and Augustus, I wondered? When they met, Livia and Augustus already had spouses. Livia was married to Tiberius Claudius Nero, her cousin. She already had a son named Tiberius, plus Livia was pregnant with a son who would be named Nero Claudius Drusus. On the other hand, Augustus had three wives in his lifetime; when he met Livia, he was married to Scribonia, a loveless and bitter political alliance. Augustus divorced her on the same day that she gave birth to their child Julia the Elder, who ended up being Augustus' only natural child. Contemporary sources claim that Augustus immediately fell in love with Livia, resulting in the two divorcing and immediately getting married. Livia soon learned how to play the role of the devoted wife and Roman matron and soon was regarded as the most powerful woman in the empire. But was their marriage happy? Though Livia claimed it was, Augustus' infidelities were well known, the couple bore no children, and political maneuvering became Livia's main passion. When Augustus died at age 75, rumors circulated that Livia had covered his figs with poison, which caused his death.

I stood in her atrium looking up at the center of the room at this figure of the cyclops who longed for love yet ended in revenge and wondered if Livia could somehow relate to that story.

After seeing the rest of Livia's home, we were led to Augustus' house, right next door. Though they had two separate apartments, the couple lived together in the latter's house, which we entered through what appeared to be a side entrance into a dark space so full of history I could almost taste it.

The first thing that struck me was red: this guy loved red on the walls and everywhere else. The second thing was the modesty of the place. This was the most powerful man in the ancient world, and yet, coming from Nero's Golden House, this seemed to be more an emperor's apartment than his primary residence. The third thing was the masks; apparently, Augustus loved the theater because the mask motif was repeated over and over.

The overuse of red in frescos probably did not have any symbolic meaning but was a popular wall color, as evidenced by the decor at Pompeii. In the 1970s, it was faux wood wall paneling that was the rage, and in Rome, at the time of Augustus, it was architectural elements and painted drapes using red. Since red is not one of my favorite colors, I longed for the blue tones in Livia's house next door.

Modesty and "gravitas" were themes that both Augustus and Livia tried to exemplify since Roman virtue was seen as the avoidance of excesses. Rather than building from scratch, Augustus purchased a house on the Palatine, which was of medium size, no marble or extravagance. It is said that he slept in the same room for forty years. He was known to brag about how simply he lived and claimed to eat only bread and cheese. Augustus also resurrected traditional social values and religious rituals, making himself Chief Priest and restoring 82 neglected temples. When Haley's comet appeared over Rome, Augustus claimed it was a sign from Julius Caesar who was blessing his reign.

*The simplicity of his furniture and household goods may be seen from couches and tables still in existence, many of which are scarcely fine enough for a private citizen. They say that he always slept on a low and plainly furnished bed.* (Suetonius, The Lives of the Caesars).[18]

The people loved him for this.

I looked around at the walls and columns and porticos, painted in reds, blues, and yellows. It was so vibrant since Italian authorities are cautious about visitors not damaging the frescos by limiting the number admitted. I was gazing at what the Emperor saw every day; I was in the room where he stood, conversed, and decided burning issues. I was here in his intimate private space, but I wanted to see more. "Let us go up to Augustus's study where he took refuge when he wanted to be alone," our guide said, inviting us to follow.

Ascending a metal stairway and gazing through a window, I was able to see that most intimate room where Augustus Caesar plotted the course of the empire or just wanted to be with his thoughts. The walls were red like blood, with geometric designs in black, green, and yellow, with fanciful winged obelisks, griffins, flowers, leaves, vases, and candelabra. This vibrant decor was in contrast to the ceiling, which was painted in lighter colors, imitating a style popular in Egypt. In the frieze on the ceiling, I spotted a winged female figure, a scary head of a satyr staring

---

18 Suetonius, The Twelve Caesars, trans. Robert Graves, ed. James Rives (London: Penguin, 2007).

at me and squiggly designs that almost looked like vines. The dominant colors were pink and white, while the other colors were of pastel shades.

I kept looking back at that crazy satyr looking down on me from Augustus' room, wondering why he chose that figure for his most intimate space. After all, the satyr, half-man, and half-beast was the nature spirit/party animal, accompanying the god of wine on his escapades, dancing with a permanent erection, and running around the forest seeking adventure. Where were the images of gods who would inspire courage, fortitude, and other Roman virtues? Why the satyr? Perhaps there was another side of Augustus to which Suetonius refers, which the masses were not privy to.

*But his amorous propensities never left him, and, as he grew older, as is reported, he was in the habit of debauching young girls, who were procured for him, from all quarters, even by his own wife.*

(C. Suetonius Tranquillus, Divus Augustus, 69).

Was the Emperor planning the expansion of the empire as he sat under the satyr's image, which was the symbol of untamed nature? Or did he come up here to get away from his wife as he made plans for rendezvous of a more sensuous nature? According to Suetonius, Livia was okay with this, as long as the public image remained untarnished.

As I descended the stairs after my visit, I wondered about the two images which dominated the private areas of Livia and Augustus. In the empress's house, Polyphemus and the sea nymph Galatea told a story of unrequited love ending in tragedy. The Emperor was gazed down on by a symbol of unbridled nature for whom drunkenness and debauchery were the norms.

Perhaps the public image of the first family as exemplars of Roman virtue was just that, an image.

# Chapter 10
# The Impoverished But Grand Lady

Franco is from Piemonte, the Turin area, and Massimo is from Lecce in Puglia. How do northern and southern Italians differ in their perspectives and experience of Rome, I wondered. Whether living in Rome for a job or family, many migrated here from other parts of Italy and brought their mentalities and cultures with them. Is Rome a dream come true or a pain in the ass? Is it something in between? I asked them.

- **Why do you live in Rome?**

**Franco.** "I've lived here for many years now because I was offered a great job opportunity."

**Massimo.** " I moved to Rome, first of all, for love and then for a job."

- **What do you like best about living in Rome?**

**Franco.** "Rome is a great city and so offers possibilities that cannot be found anywhere else. Besides this, compared with northern Italy, the city has a climate that always feels like spring."

**Massimo.** "Rome is not only the center of Italy, but it connects you to the whole world. Another thing I like about the city is Rome's beauty; its history can be seen in every angle and building. Certainly, there are negative aspects, like its dirtiness and traffic, but it is still a beautiful city."

● **Are you happy living in Rome?**

**Franco.** "In the beginning, I was happy here, but after living here for years, the disadvantages outweigh the advantages. I stay here because of my emotional ties and my work, but if I could live in another place, I would."

**Massimo.** "Yes, I am happy to be living in Rome. There are moments when I would escape, but when I am far away, I miss Rome. Though I've only lived here for a few years, I've been coming here since I was a baby because my aunt lived in Testaccio. Besides the city I was born in, I would not live in another place."

● **What is your favorite place in Rome?**

**Franco.** "My favorite area of Rome is the Aventine Hill; it is a green, peaceful place in the center of the city but seems like another world; it is rich in history yet calm and fascinating."

**Massimo.** "I find the Roman Forum to be the most interesting place in the city; I don't even know how to explain why. When I am there, I feel that I am living a life that has already been lived and yet continues; somehow, I feel part of that life flowing on that spot."

● **What functions well in Rome, and what is dysfunctional in the city?**

**Franco.** "I have to say that museums function well in Rome. Many other aspects of the city for those who live here — traffic, garbage, waiting in line — don't work well, but the museums are the exception."

**Massimo.** "It is difficult to think of something that functions well in Rome! But one thing I have to say that works well is the neighborhood fruit and vegetable sellers because their produce is fresh and the quality is always very high."

### ● What do you do with your free time in Rome?

**Franco.** "We enjoy trying to discover Rome's angles that we don't know yet, go to a museum or exhibition or just walk through the historical center. I always return home happy after taking a stroll through the center of Rome; few cities give me this satisfaction."

**Massimo.** "In my free time, I love going to a museum, an exhibition, or just walking through the city. One thing for sure, I don't spend my free time in the gym!"

### ● Can you explain the mentality that Romans have regarding rules and laws?

**Franco.** "(Chuckle). A Roman will invent his own law according to what is convenient for him."

**Massimo.** "Romans tend to disregard rules and laws; all Italians are like this, but especially Romans. Laws exist, but it is up to me to decide to follow them or not; one can see this in traffic, the work environment, the economy, etc. If a Roman perceives a law as unjust or inconvenient, he disregards it."

### ● What do you think of Romans?

**Franco.** "Romans are genuine and cheerful and have the disposition to be in a good mood. But they have the idea of 'caput mundi'[19] and this can make them a bit arrogant. Romans also have a 'papist' mentality since the Pope lives

---

19 'Head of the world.'

here. If you are part of the 'papal court,' then everything works for you, if not, then nothing does. I am commenting on the mentality, not the reality. They like to believe that they are well connected to those in power, especially those flowing from the Pope's presence.

"But Romans are also emotional people. Let me give you an example that happened: I would go to my clients in Rome (I worked in technology) to try to convince them that my product is better than the competitors' and therefore they should acquire it for their business. This was my method when I began working in Rome. But my boss, who was Roman, told me that I shouldn't go to my clients in this way, but rather that I must go to my customer with a photograph of my two children and persuade him to buy my product; otherwise my children will starve! This gives you an idea of the approach that I was told to take when dealing with clients in Rome; the relationship had to be based on an emotional response rather than analytical reasoning. This is the difference between dealing with a Roman and an Italian from the North."

**Massimo.** "I agree that Romans are jovial, full of themselves, some are civil, but they also have the quality of always saying what they think. They are genuine, and they always tell you what is in their mind; they are not false. Coming here from Lecce, I value this; those from Lecce can be more insincere but not the Romans."

"For Romans, Rome is the world, and everything else is outskirts. Centuries of history with the church's domination have created a certain 'papal court' mentality in which who you know is the way to get ahead. At times Romans seek connections with people to reach some end rather than for friendship."

- **Can you describe Rome in three words?**

**Franco.** "Beautiful, unique, and emotional."

**Massimo.** "Lady *(Signora)*, fascinating, beautiful. Rome is like a noble lady from the past; it is intriguing and beautiful, impoverished yet well dressed, overweight, covered in jewelry and makeup, and older yet still attractive.

"Rome has all the negative aspects that you can list, but if I put this on balance with its positive aspects, the positive outweighs the negative."

● **What would you like to add?**

**Massimo.** "Even though other Italian cities, such as Turin, have been the capital of Italy, Rome has the dignity and the feeling of being a national and world capital. This is striking to whoever visits here. Rome's second quality is magic: its sunsets and the way the light plays off the buildings. No other city matches the beauty of the sky and the unique light that illuminates Rome.

"Another aspect of this city is the way it embraces you; when you move here from the North or the South, you feel immediately welcome. Unlike other parts of Italy where you can be labeled as being from the South or the North, this doesn't happen in Rome. No matter where you are from, you are accepted. I never felt labeled as a southerner because Rome has embraced me."

**Franco.** "One can feel that Italy's history springs from this place and somehow a piece of each of us Italians reside in this city. Florence is beautiful but is an expression of Tuscany; Naples is an expression of the South; only Rome manifests and expresses all of us."

# Chapter 11
# Caravaggio

Inevitably my feet lead me to the church of San Luigi dei Francesi, St. Louis of the French, on a typical visit to Rome. I enter, go to the left, walk towards the main altar, stop and turn to see Caravaggio's monumental *The Calling of St. Matthew*. I find the painting riveting: its human qualities intermingled with a divine presence. I find its creator fascinating, who struggled and fought and died young, yet expressed beauty that few have been able to match.

Cardinal Ottavio Paravicino perhaps understood Caravaggio's work best when he wrote in 1603: "...some paintings were in that middle between piety and profanity, such that I would not have wished to have seen them from afar..."[20] It was in that middle ground, between the human and divine, that Caravaggio's work flourished. The unique and disastrous life of this man, who illegally carried a sword and dagger in public areas, regularly argued and fought, got into a duel with Ranuccio Tomassoni who bled to death, fled to Malta, tried to join the Order of St. John, got into another fight, got arrested, escaped, assaulted, fled again, fell ill and died at age 38; this life would be seen as a failure if

---

20 Andrew Graham-Dixon, Caravaggio: A Life Sacred and Profane (New York: W W Norton, 2012).

Caravaggio didn't paint.

As I gaze on *The Calling of St. Matthew*, I wonder at the insight of this artist with a tumultuous life. How could he look so clearly into the divine when his life was so fucked up? When he created this work, Caravaggio was getting arrested for bearing arms in public. He went around with the modern equivalent of a motorcycle gang and surrounded himself with prostitutes, courtesans, and hotheads. And yet, he achieved this! I wondered if there could be a connection.

My mind was wrapped in these thoughts as I left the church and walked over to Palazzo Madama, now the house of the Italian Senate. In the 1600s, Caravaggio lived in this building, sponsored by Cardinal Francesco Maria Del Monte; now guarded by soldiers and police, Caravaggio went in and out of this door hundreds of times with his mind full of ideas, grudges, and affections. The building, dating from 1505, sits atop the baths of Nero, right behind Piazza Navona. Now populated by the dark blue suits seen chatting outside, it was a teaming center of art and culture. Caravaggio was so proud of being part of this scene that he boasted of his patron when he got arrested: "I was arrested last night...because I was carrying a sword. I carry the sword by right because I am Painter to Cardinal del Monte. I am in his service and live in his house. I am on his household payroll." His defense didn't hold up; no matter whose service he was in, it was illegal to bear arms in public in Rome. Caravaggio often ignored this law.

The sun was setting, and I decided to walk away from the crowds and imagine I was tracing Caravaggio's footsteps. His biographers write that he often wore all black clothing, not because he was concerned about style but because he believed he could easily escape detection on the streets of Rome as he roamed the streets and alleys. As I continued, I imagined the artist stopping in one of the piazzas, meeting up with his loud and boisterous friends, stopping for a drink, singing, flashing their swords, and inspiring fear in everyone they passed. Yet, this can't be all there was to this man; he had to be an observer of life, and he had to have reflected on the meaning of events and relationships and faith; otherwise, he would not have been able to create that different world on his canvases.

It was getting dark now, as I walked the same streets that Caravaggio passed, and the images of his paintings from this period haunted me. *The Calling of St. Matthew, The Martyrdom of St. Matthew, The Conversion of St. Paul, The Crucifixion of St. Peter, The Supper at Emmaus, The Betrayal of Christ,* and the list goes on. How? How did he do it? Didn't the life he led detract from the quality of the art he produced? Or did it add to its drama and reality?

I made my way back to San Luigi di Francesi, and for some reason, the church was open that evening. I walked in again, made my way to *The Calling of St. Matthew,* and wondered. "Caravaggio," I whispered. "What were you thinking? Was this just for money or career, or did you grasp something here that the rest of us only strive for?" I looked at the hand of Christ, which seemed to mirror the position of the outstretched hand of Adam in the Sistine Chapel; somehow, you understood that Christ is the new Adam. But why is Peter standing in front of Christ, blocking him from our view? Perhaps Caravaggio imagines Peter symbolizing the Church as the visible presence of Christ in the world, and Peter, just like Christ, has his finger extended towards Matthew. Dressed in contemporary clothing and painted so large, the viewers feel like they too are seated at that table in that same room.

As I look at the figure of the Christ, his hand points, but his eyes seem to invite. The men gathered around the table each have a different reaction: one is obsessed with counting money, another is watching to make sure that the money counter isn't going to steal anything; a third looks at the scene with curiosity and the fourth man seems to look behind the two standing figures as if focused on something happening outside of the room. There is only one who takes that invitation personally, incredulously pointing to himself. "Me?" he seems to say. More than his hand pointing to himself, it is the tenderness in Mathew's eyes that are most expressive. Somehow in this encounter, Matthew feels looked at to his very core, intimately known, which generates a sense of surprise and a bond with the one who looked at him with love and mercy. Matthew seems both moved and astonished because of that encounter that we are witnessing take place in his money sorting room. Caravaggio's scene is more than a painting; it is an invitation to enter a different world.

The next morning I had a burning desire to try to understand Caravaggio further, so I made my way to Piazza del Popolo to witness another encounter that the artist captured. It was the *Conversion on the Way to Damascus*, in the Chiesa di Santa Maria del Popolo, or Church of St. Mary of the People. Could this painting shed light on this man's double life, a ruffian and sublime artist?

Upon entering, I noticed that Santa Maria del Popolo's interior looks like any other ugly baroque church, like somebody vomited dark marble and gold everywhere, one's eyes not knowing where to rest. I made my way through the baroque jungle to the Cerasi Chapel in search of the artist and stepped into a world greater than mine: there hung *The Conversion on the Way to Damascus*, a work so full of surprise and astonishment that I had to sit down to try to absorb it. Here was a man on the ground, St. Paul, who had overseen the persecution of the new Christian sect and who had stood by and supported St. Stephen's execution in 36 CE taking place before his eyes. Here was this same man, certain of himself and his convictions, willing to judge and condemn those whose ways differed from his, whose own moral uprightness went unquestioned; now this man was on the ground, fallen from his horse, eyes closed, overcome by something. His sword of persecution now on the ground, the man reaches up to embrace something that he cannot see but knows is there. The viewer is brought into the event by that sweet light which bathes the scene in comfort. He has fallen from his horse, his eyes blinded, yet his face is calm. What did Caravaggio see in this scene that I can't quite perceive?

"Saul, Saul, why do you persecute me?"

"Who are you, Lord?" The biblical account of the event

states. The bleakness of the painting contrasts with the church's flamboyant decoration, as Paul's body seems outstretched beyond the canvas. "Who are you?" he asks as he reaches up. "I am Jesus who you are persecuting," was the response. With these words, Paul's entire moral outlook came crashing down. By not associating with thieves, prostitutes, and foreigners, he was doing God's work, he had believed. By judging those who did not respect the Torah's teachings, he was carrying out God's will. He was so sturdy, so sure, so incapable of empathy; yet, here he was, on his back, arms reaching up.

Somehow Caravaggio grasped what mattered: not the ornateness, not the sword, not his moral preconceptions, not his way of life, not riches, not his plans and goals. What Paul experienced in that encounter became what was most important to him, and Caravaggio somehow understood that. It was that relationship with the divine that began to transform Paul that day and made his life become a vessel through which that same soft light could bathe others.

My quest for the real Caravaggio was not yet complete. Still, somehow, leaving Santa Maria del Popolo, I felt that below his acerbic nature in Caravaggio's heart, a divine spark burned.

# Chapter 12
## People Watching

The entire world comes to Rome, and if I cannot visit each country, I can at least get a sense of its people if I stay in the city long enough. When I was a student in Rome, I recall that the Syrians were very competitive (they loved to organize ping pong tournaments), the Nigerians were outgoing, and the French were the most serious. Overall impressions do not define a person since there were exceptions, but certain traits are observable that are more prevalent in one culture than in another. I had this in mind when I sat at a cafe in Piazza Navona with my friend Ted one sunny afternoon; we ordered a few beers, started observing and soon after began making judgments.

"You think those two are gay?" I asked. "Is the Pope Catholic?" Ted responded. I took another sip. A minute later, our view was blocked by a group of Japanese tourists, wearing red baseball hats, following a guide holding up a closed umbrella. "You'd think she could at least buy a flag," I remarked. Ted nodded as the crowd passed by, casting shadows on us. The group seemed at first to be dozens, but the procession didn't stop. "That must be a great tour experience with half the population on it," Ted said. The stragglers were towards the end of the group, jostling to get closer to the front as if their lives depended on it. "Why are they so stressed out?" Ted asked as I shrugged.

"Two points for picking out Americans," I said. "Three if they are across the piazza," Ted added. "American at 3 o'clock," I said, as we turned to see an older man dressed in a Hawaiian shirt, with his wife, just entering the area. "American at 1 o'clock," Ted called out as we spied a college-aged man walking next to the fountain wearing an MIT T-shirt. "OK, I get points for all those girls," I said, as a group of teenaged girls sat down on the railing surrounding Bernini's fountain. "Looks like they all bought their shorts at the same store," I continued. "Two gay Americans at 6 o'clock," Ted called out as we turned and saw two men, somewhat muscular, dressed in tank tops. I nodded; "Awww, the tell-tale tank top." "American family!" I called out, as a trinket seller approached husband, wife, and two kids and offered to sell his trinket for 5 euros rather than the 1 he sells to everyone else for. "You're good," Ted commented, nodding. A moment later, a group of 6 tourists rode into the piazza on Segways; we turned to each other and said simultaneously: "Americans!"

Time for another beer and series of judgment calls.

Near us were several African men with blankets on the ground; one had handbags for sale, another wood carvings and a third was selling sunglasses and hats. "Wow, I wonder how they live," Ted said with compassion. As we watched, the sellers tried to engage the passerby in conversation. "Where are you from?" they asked. "I have something nice for you," said the other seller. Most continued to walk, a few stopped to look at the goods, but nobody was buying. "I give you a good price," said the handbag seller to a woman walking away. "You can only imagine what they were escaping from in their country to come here and try to live off what they sell on the streets," Ted continued. As we gazed at them, there was a sudden commotion; another African called out from across the piazza. The police were approaching rapidly. The sellers suddenly threw their goods inside their sheets, gathered up the ends, and ran in the opposite direction. Another policeman had been hiding behind a building; he stepped out and caught one of the Africans, demanding to see his papers, while the other two disappeared. Soon the other officers arrived and surrounded the man, who had a terrified look on his face. As they continued to demand his papers, they led him away and out of sight.

It only took a few minutes for the atmosphere in Piazza Navona to return to festive. Soon the King Tut impersonator began setting up his area in front of us: he placed his block of wood, slipped into his Pharaoh costume, put his mask on, and mounted his riser in the hope of getting change thrown into his little basket in front of him. Nobody even looked at him, so he began to wave to tourists but still no change. I've seen this man in Rome over the past five or six years and cannot imagine how he survives. Just then, a Dominican, a priest dressed in the white robe of that order, walked by, and I wondered what his life looked like compared to this Pharaoh. The Dominican was perhaps a professor at a local university, lived in a convent with his brother Dominicans, interacted with people who had problems and doubts and dreams; because of his identity, he could penetrate their intimate realms. Perhaps he started in Spain or Portugal or an unknown village in Chile; he ended up in Rome, in this place, crossing this piazza. Then there was the Pharaoh, day after day, year after year, standing on that block of wood. Was he doing this from necessity? What choices did he make that made him end up here, on that block of wood? The Dominican passing in front of him perhaps came from across the world, was studying, teaching, working with people while the Pharaoh stood still waiting for coins. I don't know their story, but it was curious to see these two so different lives come within 3 feet of one another without either of them taking notice.

We could see St. Agnes, the beautiful baroque church facing the Bernini Fountain, from where we were sitting. Around the entrance were gathering Spanish youth together with a young priest. They were setting up signs and started parading around the piazza; the signs said something about Jesus and salvation. They seemed very enthusiastic as they tried to shepherd bystanders into the church; the priest played guitar as the youths began singing. I looked at Ted and rolled my eyes. "Well, I can see they want to bring their faith into the streets and not just stay in church all day," Ted said, thoughtfully. I nodded. "Yeah, that's what Pope Francis has been trying to do: get the priests and religious people into the world, get their hands dirty, and bring hope. I see that, but this seems silly to me," I said, as a group of singing Spanish youth, led by their priest, skipped in front of us.

We were on our third beer and decided to get something to eat to offset the alcohol. "Due lasagne per favore,"[21] I said to our waiter as we scanned the piazza once more.

An African couple passed in front of us, traditional dress, apparently wealthy. "Nigeria," I stated, and Ted agreed. He was dressed in a shimmering light blue robe, and on his head, he wore a flat grey hat. "He looks like a movie star!" I commented. His wife wore a long dark blue robe with a matching headdress and pearls around her neck. They looked like they stepped out of Vogue. Ted looked and raised his eyebrows as they walked past, chatting in English. "I wonder how many yachts they own?" Ted asked. "They break our stereotype about Africa being destitute," I added. "Well, Nigeria has one of the world's highest economic growth rates, though roughly a third of its population lives in poverty. Don't ask me how I know that!" Ted said.

Our lasagna arrived, and the sun was starting to set, turning the piazza into a golden hue. The group of jazz musicians who were here nightly started setting their instruments up, three gypsies sauntered by, looking this way and that. There was a large group from India, two American seminarians with their rosaries, a completely veiled Muslim woman and her husband, smiling families with small children, another large tourist group, a man and his dog, a woman and her baby in a stroller…. We were too busy eating to make any comments.

An American family came and sat at the table next to us as we finished our delicious pasta, wiping our mouths, sipping our beers, we were content. "Well, everybody has their story," I said. "And few live up to the stereotypes we judge them by," Ted

---

21 "Two orders of lasagna please."

added. "Some stories are sad, others happy or mixed; some are of poverty and fleeing violence, others of abundance and enjoyment. But nobody's story is simple, and this piazza is full of the crisscrossing of stories and lives and drama and dreams from all over the world," I said. Ted nodded. "And nobody is predictable. We should be careful about how we judge; just because someone is from a certain country doesn't mean that they are going to act in a certain way," he added.

Just then, we overheard the family behind us place their order: "Five coca colas. And do you serve hamburgers here?"

# Chapter 13
## Lesser Visited Rome:
## Palazzo Altemps and Ostia Antica

I was tired of the mobs of tourists everywhere, so I decided to seek out lesser-visited Rome. No Coliseum, Forum, or Vatican for me today; I headed over to the Altemps Museum behind Piazza Navona.

The Altemps Palace is part of the National Museum of Rome, located in four locations, including the Altemps; tourists usually skip this museum, having limited time and much to see. I was lucky that morning I walked in and bought a ticket since there was no line; in fact, I had the whole museum to myself.

I stepped into the courtyard of the fifteenth-century palace and turned a slow circle as I gazed at Renaissance arches, porticos, and ancient sculptures. There were four huge statues in front of me; I was surprised that they were exposed to the elements. Of the four, the one that stood out was the "Resting Athlete"; I walked over and stood in front of this almost living piece of stone. The body was rough, but the face was smooth, perhaps betraying a Renaissance-era restoration; however, the power of the statue remained. Massive legs holding up a rippled muscular body, enormous chest and bulging biceps; yet the athlete, one leg raised, looks up as if reflecting. This figure was no muscle head; this was capturing the Renaissance, and the ancient ideal of man fully developed physically, mentally, and emotionally. I circled and walked behind to see the backside of our athlete, and I was not disappointed. Returning to the front, I realized that this statue spoke to me about the grandeur of humanity, which the ancients hinted at and the Renaissance humanists fully embraced. Here was depicted the dignity of humankind.

I walked under the heavily frescoed portico, which was lined with boring busts of emperors; I propped up my phone and took a selfie among the emperors with an expression that I owned the world too. I then decided to explore the museum without worrying about logic or chronology; let my feet take the lead.

The first sculpture that beckoned me was a robed woman with a half robed young man; it appeared to be a teacher and her student. The woman was gazing into the youth's eyes, one arm around his shoulder and the other touching his arm. It seemed to be an innocent statement about the bonds between students and educators. But as I approached the sculpture, I was able to read its title: Orestes and Electra. I paused as I recalled the story, which was far more sinister than my first interpretation.

Orestes and Electra were the children of King Agamemnon and his wife, Clytemnestra. While her husband was away at the Trojan War, Clytemnestra nursed her grudge against Agamemnon, who had sacrificed his daughter Iphigenia to gain the god's favor for the war. Clytemnestra aligned herself with Agamemnon's cousin Aegisthus, who became her lover. The two of them plotted and carried out Agamemnon's murder in revenge for the daughter's killing, for which Clytemnestra never forgave her husband. After her mother murdered her father, Electra believed that her brother Orestes was in danger, since Aegisthus, her mother's lover, would not want a son of Agamemnon to be in line for the throne. Fearing for her brother Orestes's life, Electra sent him away with his tutor, where he could be out of harm's way. Once Orestes grew from boy to man, he hatched a plot to return to avenge his father by slaying his mother Clytemnestra and her lover Aegisthus and claim his throne.

Orestes planned to enter the palace with his friend Pylades, disguised as messengers carrying an urn, which they would claim were the remains of Orestes who they would say was dead. Electra had always mourned the death of her father, King Agamemnon, and had never forgiven her mother; when she heard of Orestes' "death," she was overcome with grief. Orestes did not recognize his sister Electra when he handed her the urn, nor did she know him. She began to lament the death of her beloved brother, with Orestes standing in front of her, who then realized this was his sister Electra. The sculpture in the Altemps museum captures that moment when brother and sister are reunited.

The story continues that Orestes and Pylades slew Clytemnestra in the palace and waited to kill Aegisthus on the spot where Agamemnon was murdered.

So the benign statuary group that I had believed was a teacher and student was the midpoint in a story of revenge and retribution.

I continued my museum adventure and almost walked into a clamoring, emotional, and violent battle scene. It was the *Ludovisi Battle Sarcophagus*, standing proudly against a wall. I could practically hear the cries, the clanging of shields, and the sound of horses in battle as I took my place in front of the writhing bodies jumping out of the front of the sarcophagus. It was too much to take in, so I approached the carving to examine one section at a time.

The Romans are the figures with noble expressions dressed in soldiers' gear, whereas the Goths have distorted faces and dressed in cloths and rags. Layers of straining horses and twisted bodies make it difficult to focus on one point, just how it must be in battle. But on the right side of the sarcophagus there is a Goth grasping the leg of a Roman, asking to be spared. The Roman has his sword raised as he grabs the hair of his captive, ready to cut his throat; there is no mercy on his face.

My eyes are carried to the bottom half of the sarcophagus where the ground is littered with the bodies of the Goths who are falling, being stepped on, trampled over and subjected to Roman might. On the left half, however, amid this turmoil, there is a different scene of stillness: a Roman soldier with a stern expression standing in front of a kneeling Goth, with a bulbous nose and pleading eyes. The soldier has his hand under the Goth's chin and the other hand around his neck, looking in his eyes. It is the moment of a moral decision: to spare this man or kill him. All the tumult around the pair does not infringe on this moment of quiet decision: what is the right thing to do? We do not know what the soldier decided, but we are witnessing that instant as he weighed his options.

The sarcophagus center is the soldier on the horse, with an outstretched arm and serene expression. With the battle raging around him, this man is calm; he must be the deceased since he is the only one untouched by the struggle surrounding him. Holding neither sword nor shield, with cape swirling around him as if it were wings, the man's arm beckons to the viewer to behold the combat as he emerges triumphant. It is unsure who this figure represents, though some say the young general depicted was the son of Emperor Decius, named Hostilian, who died of the plague but whose father died in a battle against a federation of Scythians under the command of a Gothic King. Whether the man at the center is Hostilian or another, it is clear that he is invincible (not wearing a helmet), serene and in control. There is an indentation on his forehead in the form of an X, which may refer to the Mithraic cult, a popular religion among Roman soldiers. The X and the outstretched arm could signify both a farewell and a belief in the afterlife with the god Mithras, who the soldier has served faithfully.

"Goodbye, faithful soldier," I whisper as I turn to explore the other parts of the room.

I had avoided looking at the monumental sculpture in the center while I was heading over to the sarcophagus because I didn't want to spoil the surprise. But now I retraced my steps, head down, repositioned myself, and looked up; I found myself in front of the monumental and amazing *The Galatian Suicide*, which grabbed me by the throat and heart as I stood there staring.

Here was a man with a defiant look on his face, holding up his wife, who he had just slain; poised to plunge his sword into his chest, he chose death for himself and his spouse rather than slavery. It is a Roman copy of a third-century BCE Greek bronze original, which depicts the defeat of the Galatians by Attalus I in 223 BCE. As I circled to get a better view of the Gaul's face, his expression was striking; he seemed filled with courage, strength, and determination. He would not allow his enemies to take their prize and was not afraid to plunge his sword into his body. His wife was clothed for modesty, but the Gaul was nude, a sign of fearlessness. His ideal body is twisted as blood already spurts from his chest, where the sword has entered. It is not a sculpture glorifying suicide or death but rather the dignity of freedom and the determination of one's destiny. "You shall NOT have your way with me," I could almost hear him utter.

I stood there in silence for a while, alone in the room with the Gaul and his dead wife; words failed, my thoughts stilled as I looked and looked. After about 30 minutes, I walked out, feeling as if I had just witnessed something momentous.

I was done with museums for the day and decided to return to Palazzo Altemps another time to see the rest of the collection. I was filled up and satisfied, so I hopped a bus and then a train to make my way to another little-visited location, Ostia Antica, which held the ruins of Ostia's ancient Roman port city.

I expected to find a few rocks and fallen columns among the weeds with maybe a few low walls if I was lucky. But as I paid my entrance fee and stepped inside of Ostia Antica, I was shocked: after a path lined with ancient tombs, there were complete buildings (minus the roofs), arches, and streets. This place was almost as impressive as Pompeii but minus the distance! After a morning in a museum, it was refreshing to be outdoors and still in the ancient world.

I had a plan in Ostia since I wanted to explore the Mithraic temples first; I had heard that sixteen of them had been found thus far, and I was fascinated by this religion, which was, for many Romans, the precursor to Christianity.

I soon stumbled across the Baths of Mithras and down a flight of stairs, almost hidden, was the Mithraic temple or Mithraeum. It was dark, resembling a cave, with a dramatic statue of Mithras slaying the bull, from whose blood the universe came forth. There were stone benches on the sides where the participants sat, two skylights illuminating the statue, a cold brick floor, and an eerie atmosphere. I sat down on one of these benches in the exact place where a soldier sat as he listened to the seven steps and virtues of the Mithraic way explained by the *Pater* or Father. Once the bull's slaying was reenacted, this same soldier would have had the blood smeared on his forehead, linking purification with the sacrifice of a life, followed by a feast of unity by all initiates present and an oath of loyalty to keep their fellowship sacred. No wonder that Christianity spread so quickly in Rome since many of its beliefs ran parallel to Mithraism.

It was time to discover another Mithraeum so, after climbing out of that dark hole, I made my way in another direction but soon spied the amphitheater, which I had to stop at and investigate.

Before climbing the theatre stairs, I paused at the sign, which explained that the structure dates from the first century and initially held 3,000 spectators. In the second century, it was enlarged and could seat 4,000; the theatre's building and renovations are attributed to Emperors Septimius Severus, Caracalla, and Commodus. I looked up at the structure, and it almost looked too perfect, perhaps due to more recent renovations. But many of the bricks and stones were authentic, and that was good enough for me as I climbed the stairs to take in the view.

It was that post-pranzo hour when many Italians were at home, and many tourists were feeling the weight of the day; I heard Americans and Germans chatting as I approached the top tier and sat down to take in the scene. The semicircular theatre faced a grove of umbrella pines where there was once the back wall of the stage, dismantled/looted for its marble. I imagined the roar or laughing of the crowd as they participated in comedies or reenactments of mythological tales. There is some evidence that the stage area was flooded; it would not have been deep enough for a mock naval battle as in the Colosseum but would have been sufficient if there was a story taking place in the water, such as the birth of Venus or a tale involving sirens and sea nymphs.

Since Ostia was a port city, the audience must have been international, just like the foreigners poking through the ruins and wandering across the stage area today. The theatre was the center of entertainment for the Romans and could range from the heights of Greek tragedy to the depths of gladiatorial combat. Ostia was no different, and perhaps the spectacles presented were more international, less cultural, and more appealing to a multitude of backgrounds.

It was time to stop daydreaming and start snooping, so I got up and walked down the stone stairs to see what remnants of theatre life I could still find. Behind where the stage wall once stood, there were giant weird marble masks which were probably part of the stage decoration and resembled those worn by actors. Grotesque expressions, huge eyes, and big mouths enabled the actors to switch characters without the audience knowing it was the same actor; men could play a hero or slave, a mistress or nymph, a monster, or a king.

I stood on the stage area and looked up into the crowd, now consisting of about a dozen tourists milling around. Should I cry out some verses from Sophocles to see how far my voice would reach? I decided not to recite but instead imagine an actor on that same stage, with mask and wig, looking up onto those crowded bleachers as they were engaged in a tragedy or comedy, bringing the story to life with their voices and gestures. I imagined that it was *Oedipus the King* being performed. The crowd was silent with anticipation as the curse of Oedipus unfolded; it was a tale they would have been familiar with, but to see it on stage, the actors bringing the story to life, must have been breathtaking. As Oedipus realizes that he unwittingly killed his father and married his mother, the audience, horrified at the unfolding of the curse, must have held their breath not to miss one word of the dialogue. Here I was, standing in perhaps that same place where that actor stood who was playing out the tragedy of Oedipus as if it were his own as he held the audience in the palm of his hand. This stage where I now stood was an analogy which Shakespeare captured centuries later:

*All the world's a stage, and all the men and women merely players: they have their exits and their entrances, and one man in his time plays many parts, his acts being seven ages.*

(Shakespeare, As You Like It.).

The actors who stood here and the thousands of spectators who sat in that audience each played many parts: citizens and freedmen, fathers and sons, daughters and mothers, workers and politicians, sailors and business owners; each had their story and their opportunities to do good and evil and everything in between. They had made their exits, the audience had dispersed, the stage had been dismantled, and the theatre had fallen into decay.

I still wanted to see at least one more Mithraeum before leaving Ostia, so I made my way in the direction that I thought most likely, I would find one.

I soon came across the Mithraeum of Felicissimus, of which little remains except for a magnificent mosaic floor, which traces the seven degrees of initiation into Mithraism. As I stood at the entrance and looked down, the designs included a small well and other symbols: a large vase, symbolizing water, an altar with a burning fire, symbolizing sacrifice to the god, and two caps with two stars on top, symbolizing the twin brothers Castor and Pollux, who probably represent the two celestial hemispheres. So right away, the symbolism connects me to the essential elements of water, fire, and air (the celestial sphere). Mithraism is a cult that had its belief system rooted in the cosmos; the sun was the symbol of Mithras, and the signs of the zodiac were the sun god's associates. Though worshiped in a cave, Mithras beckoned his followers to look out and to make sense of the universe through their belief system.

I wanted to experience these initiation steps in my mind as I looked at the first square where there were three figures: the raven who was the messenger to Mithras at the beginning of his mission, a scepter, which is a symbol of Mercury, the messenger of the gods, and a small cup, a symbol of an offering. At this stage, the initiate wore a raven's mask; since the raven can fly, this step is connected with the air, and the ordeals that the initiate had to pass through may have involved rituals associated with this element.

The second square is damaged, but I could make out a bit of a torch, a diadem, and a lamp. This second stage is the strange initiation step in which the participant would "wed" himself to the god; the wedding torch, the diadem referring to the goddess Venus and the lamp, meaning that now the initiate could bring the god's light into the world. In this step, the initiate formed a closer and more intimate relationship with the god Mithras and became his instrument.

Mithraism was extremely popular among the empire soldiers, so it is easy to imagine that this initiation step was a favorite. "Miles" or soldier was the name of this phase, and its symbolism on the mosaic includes the soldier's tools: lance, helmet, and soldier's kit bag. The "Miles" were under the patronage of Mars, the god of war; they made the oath to serve the gods in battle and to give Mithras all the glory. The ritual connected with this step included offering a wreath to the soldier; once the *Pater* or father placed it on the soldier's head, the initiate would push it off with his hand and declare that Mithras alone is his wreath. Strength, courage, and humility are qualities of this step.

The symbols of the fourth step here are just plain weird: a fire shovel, a lightning bolt, and a sistrum, a musical instrument from ancient Egypt. Other Mithraeums have a more explicit connection of the fourth step to the lion, who had a fiery nature and whose symbol was the fire shovel, with the thunderbolt referring to Jupiter. There are references that the fourth stage initiates purified their hands and tongues with honey, avoiding water, which was seen as the opposite of fire. The lion and lightning bolt also symbolize the end of the world, which will be destroyed by fire according to Mithraic transcriptions, but the just would be spared. In this fourth step, the initiative worked towards his salvation.

In the fifth panel are the sword, crescent moon, scythe, and evening star; these are Persian symbols, which refers to the origin of this cult. This initiate grade is under the protection of the moon; honey is again used in this ritual but is seen as a preservation agent, keeping food fresh during the long winter months. The Persians believed that honey came from the moon, where the semen of the bull slain by Mithras was brought and purified. The scythe is the symbol of the keeper of the fruits and the one who watches over the land's bounty.

As we approach the highest levels of this mystery religion, the symbols of a whip, a radiate halo, and a torch appear, signifying Heliodromus, the Courier of the Sun. The sun crosses the sky in his chariot, driving the horses forward with his whip, and the initiate, at this stage, becomes the sun god's earthly representative. At this stage, the follower of Mithras is called to the highest form of virtue and an example to his fellow soldiers and initiates as he brings the creative force of the god to his companions. The rituals connected with this level include the slaying of a bull, the participation in the sacred meal, and the wearing of a red robe and yellow belt, signifying membership in a mystical community.

The final and highest level is that of *Pater* or Father, from which, perhaps, the Catholic Church derives the concept. He was the shepherd of his Mithraeum, responsible for initiates of all levels and for recruiting new members. His responsibility was to safeguard and impart the mysteries and to interpret the teachings of the god. He was called to be a father to all, supreme teacher and defender of his flock. The symbols of this level are the Phrygian cap of Mithras, referring to its Persian origins; the staff, symbolizing a shepherd, the sickle of Saturn who watched over the *Pater* and the paten or offering plate, referring to sacrifice to the god.

The final panel is simply the guy who funded this Mithraeum, named Felicissimus, who wanted to be remembered. Thank you, Felicissimus.

I had come to Ostia Antica to see the sixteen Mithraeums; instead, I saw two; plus I visited the amphitheater. This experience was part of the magic: I could let the city guide me rather than imposing myself on it.

The sun was going down, my mind was tired, and it was time to head back to Rome.

# Chapter 14
# Is it *Dolce Vita* After All? Expats

Rome is full of expats who come to the city for a career, on a whim, or for love. Each expat has his/her own story and experience of the city. This begins to paint a picture of how a foreigner feels in this international place. Does Rome ultimately measure up? I asked a few expats to tell me their story.

Maazouza is a 37-year-old woman from Algeria who immigrated to Rome. Rachel fell in love with Italy and is a chef from the United States. Kevin works in real estate in Rome and is originally from Southern California.

● **Can you tell me your story?**

**Rachel.** "I am a baker and chef in America, so I spend most of my time observing the food and hospitality of the Italian people. I have a lot of free time to read and think and walk around, and I have noticed a change in my inner self. My heart is more tender since moving here, and I did not expect that to happen. In the beginning, I took the advice of my Zia to 'never smile at anyone'! But now I feel more sincere affection for people who I love. When I am back in the US, I notice how much I miss getting so many kisses on the cheek. It truly changes the dynamic of the day when your friends and family kiss you; what a beautiful thing that we have tragically lost in the States."

**Maazouza.** "Since I am the only girl, leaving home and traveling was not an option for me, not even in my dreams.

I thought the only way to get out of Algeria was through education; I didn't have any idea how to leave, but I felt that I deserved a better place to live, a better life.

"After high school, I had to choose my university major; I wanted something related to sports, but my family was opposed to it because they said that a female working in the sports field was against our culture. So I asked my family to choose my field so I wouldn't have to argue with anyone. They decided that I should go to study midwifery because it would be the only profession that would keep me far away from men.

"After specializing in midwifery, I saw my opportunity to leave Algeria, since there was no work near my home. I first moved to Dubai and worked in a clinic where I learned about insurance, healthcare technology, and other skills. But during these years, I dreamed of living in Europe to continue my education; I applied many times, but I was rejected in Spain, Hungary, Germany, and France; I have no idea why I was not accepted. I then decided that I would apply for a student visa one last time, and I would not apply again if I didn't get accepted this time. You can imagine my joy when I obtained a student visa for Italy! Finally, my dream came true! So I resigned from my job in Dubai, packed my things, and began my new journey in Rome. I arrived in October of 2016 when I started my master's degree as well as learning Italian. It was difficult for me to find a job, perhaps because I wore a scarf, so I took another course in Cultural Mediation since I speak three languages; this led me to assist new immigrants in assimilating. After this course and the completion of my diploma, I obtained my present job at an Immigration Detention Center."

**Kevin.** "I came here without a penny, but I didn't want to be a housewife. I started by selling tickets in front of the coliseum; I hated it, but it was a start. I worked as a bartender briefly. Then I found an American looking for a salesperson to be like a real estate agent to rent apartments to expats. I jumped right in, and she took the opportunity and returned to the US and never came back. So I grew the business, renting out to UN and NATO people; eventually, I quit and started my own company. I manage apartments and rent out to professionals; I don't even advertise; it is by word of mouth. I rent out short and long term apartments and have built a successful business. My husband, being from Trastevere, was my key; he opened so many doors. So my story began here humbly, standing in front of the coliseum chasing down tourists, and now we have built up our life."

### • Why did you move to Rome?

**Maazouza.** "I ended up in Rome because I wanted to make a new and independent life."

**Rachel.** "I did not expect to move to Rome because I just came here for a visit. I booked a one-way ticket because I was unsure how long I would stay and where I would go next. (I still am unsure of these things more than one year later) but I keep returning to Rome because I feel more like myself than anywhere else I have lived."

**Kevin.** "I am from Los Angeles, and I came here because my husband is from Rome; the reasons we moved here include: we couldn't survive in the US with only one of us working, healthcare in Italy is affordable, and my husband could never fit in since he never learned English."

### • Why do you stay in Rome?

**Maazouza.** "Now, I have a job here and a life, my life, after such a long time fighting for it."

**Rachel.** "Rome is addicting for me. I find myself more intrigued by it, the longer I am here. It is challenging to meet people and understand the city's undercurrent, including the art and the vibe. I think this challenge keeps me from leaving."

**Kevin.** "Being in Rome exposes you to the world, which is the amazing thing about living in this city."

- **What do Romans think of you?**

**Kevin.** "I'm an exception because I am not white. I am Filipino, so many Italians think that I clean houses. When I tell them I'm a statistician with a Ph.D., they don't understand. Then they discover I am American, and they forget I am Filipino, and then they tend to think that I am Japanese.

"There is a certain racism in Rome that I have seen: I walk into a bar with my driver and see the difference in how they talk to him and talk to me. They address him as if he is a lowlife. It is a type of racism, but Italian racism is different from the US. For example, the term for a house cleaner here is "Filipino"; they may ask, "Do you know a Filipino? I need someone to clean my house." It's offensive, but they are not aware of it. Romans are friendly people, that's the odd thing. It's not mean racism but is another type that is difficult to define."

- **What is the funniest thing that happened to you since moving here?**

**Rachel.** "I suppose getting picked up at a random train station by a friend of a friend who had a donkey in his truck."

- **What do you like the most about living in Rome?**

**Kevin.** "I love the food, I value the culture, and I love that it is cheaper than in Los Angeles. The food is more affordable, accessing culture is more economical, the cost of living is cheaper.

"I'm from southern California where we have the ghetto system: if you cross the street, it can become a bad neighborhood. I was born in Glendale, and I was destined to stay there. But when I moved to Hollywood, I was amazed to meet so many different types of people. Rome is like Hollywood on steroids. You might live next door to a pauper, a countess, or an extremely wealthy family on the same street. Many noble families don't have any money; we employ a countess to do our laundry. She has a greater title than another countess I know who is wealthy, so the rich countess should, according to etiquette, kiss our laundress's hand."

- **Is it possible to start from nothing and build up a life here?**

**Kevin.** "I started from nothing and built up a business here, and now I make about six times as much as a typical Italian. It only takes goals and determination."

- **What is the most frustrating thing about living in Rome?**

**Kevin.** "Some Romans I know don't have any discipline because they think they can get away with things. They know that everything will be OK, they are sheltered, they tend not to care about appointments or getting things done. They know they won't lose their jobs; if a customer complains, they won't lose their employment.

"The most frustrating thing is the hospital system here; in Florence, it works, but in Rome, it doesn't. Now Romans, like my husband, don't seem to care. But I am extremely offended by the way they do things. When I am offended that someone slights him, I look at him, and he just says: 'That's the way it works!' Doctors are looking at their phones when treating a patient, being distracted, not focused; I get offended by this, but Romans just shrug.

"Another frustrating thing is asking for a permit; it is an impossible task. If a building is registered, there are layers of laws protecting it. When you call a government agency, every time you call, you get a different answer to your question because the person answering the phone doesn't have the authority to give you an answer, but they will tell you anything just to get you off the phone. After you finish your renovation, you discover that you are being fined for breaking an Italian law that you didn't know about.

"I just don't pay these fines, and there aren't any consequences since Rome is so disorganized. I've neglected to pay traffic fines, and nothing ever happens. But the Italian equivalent of the IRS is the most efficient agency."

### • Tell me about the Italian mentality that you have encountered here.

**Rachel.** "I love how the mentality of Italian people forms concentric circles around food. I love hearing people talk about what they will cook for dinner, asking friends if they enjoy that particular dish. They chat about what they ate for lunch, what they ordered from the restaurant, what was served at a party, and the slight variations in how everyone makes dishes with the same ingredients. I love how, if you are over someone's house during a mealtime, there is a place set for you at the table, no questions asked."

**Kevin.** "In the mentality here, no doesn't mean no. For example, at their Department of Motor Vehicles, they may tell you no, but you argue and explain, and they will eventually find a way to help you. This ambiguity is because a large percentage of the population was historically poor, so there is the mentality to help each other out.

"To get something done in Rome, you have to know somebody who knows somebody; you can't bribe your way through things. When you get caught, that's when you bribe; this is the case not only in dealing with the government but hospitals or any institution. It works this way because those who work in these places know they won't get fired no matter what, so they don't work very hard. Their unions are so strong, so they aren't motivated. But if you know someone, they are more apt to get things done for you. You see this all over the place: if you see five men working on the streets, one is working, and the others are chatting. You can't even get mad at them because they are so nice and personable.

"Romans whom I know like to spend a lot of time talking about how their government doesn't work. The only time something worked well in Italian history is when they've had a dictatorship. All the straight streets were built by either the king or Mussolini. I'm not saying to let a dictator take over, but it almost takes a central authority to get things organized.

"But if someone would ask me 'Do you want to live in a place like Milan, where everything works, or Rome?', if I had to choose, I would always select Rome because people are friendly in Rome. There is more to life than meeting your deadline.

"In the US, things work because most people follow the law; you can see this in the way we drive. In Italy, you have to be smart enough to make the traffic laws work for you; if you don't, the people in the back of you will be upset.

"Here, you can bend the rules, but you have to be considerate; you have to know when you're going too far. If you're bothering somebody, then you don't bend the rules."

- **What is dating like in Rome?**

**Rachel.** "Dating in Rome is a bit like time traveling: gender-norms are still in full effect. In some ways, this is comforting, but in others, it is oppressive. It's like being inside of a Fellini film."

- **Can you tell me about Roman men?**

**Maazouza.** "Most Roman men are handsome, nice faces with nice physiques, but most of them have limited economic resources, so they struggle with rent and monthly fees. In general, they are gentlemen and are excellent chefs."

**Kevin.** "Roman men have a macho thing going on; they have this facade of behaving a certain way which goes for gay and straight Italian men. In Rome's gay world, you have extremes: you have the flamboyant and the super macho.

"I think it's an Anglo-Saxon thing to say: 'when you're straight, you're straight.' That doesn't hold here. When you're straight, you're not really straight; you could sleep with a guy even if you're married. But *bella figura*, appearances, are essential: in Rome, closeted gay men wouldn't hang out publicly with gay people because they don't want to be outed.

"Some Roman men I know are whiny about everything; their health, the government, their day. It's part of the culture; *if you cry, the fruit will come*, according to one of their sayings, so if you complain enough, good things will come. If you ask a business owner how business is, he will tell you how horrible it is. They never tell you that things are great."

- **Can you tell me about Italian women?**

**Maazouza.** "To me, Italian ladies are less pretty than men, and many of those I have met are lesbians. Also, they can be kind but are sometimes racist."

**Rachel.** "Italian women are the decision-makers; they hold life together for everyone else."

**Kevin.** "Italian women are beautiful, some of the most beautiful women I've seen. When they're young, they eat a massive bowl of spaghetti, and they are still slim and elegant! Where does it all go? They have hollow legs! Some women friends of mine struggle because, once they hit 30, they are not so beautiful and find it frustrating. Even the beautiful ones, my women friends tell me that they are sex-starved; they find Roman men uninteresting. Chivalry is alive here with definite male/female roles, even in driving.

"Roman women are like gay men in women's bodies; that's why it is easy to get along with them! We love to complain, and we get all bitchy, and we laugh a lot about things that don't go our way!

"But I do have to say that Roman women know how to dress and look good when they age; it is not unusual to see a woman in her 80s dressed well and in heels. Also, I would say that Roman women have a capacity for empathy and caring that I haven't seen everywhere."

• **If someone is thinking about moving to Rome, what would you tell them?**

**Maazouza.** "If someone is very organized and is used to high standards in customer service, then Rome is not your place."

**Kevin.** "If you are thinking of moving to Rome, just do it. It is easy to move here from the US. Just come, don't hesitate. Make sure you don't bring everything with you. I left everything back home. Don't make it easy to go back home.

"Come with only your luggage; if you are American, you can get ahead immediately. In China, they would hire a white person in an office, which would give clients a sense of importance. It is the same here; there is a certain class system where doors open if you're American. For example, I have never gotten an Italian driver's license, and when I get caught, I just say: "What? I didn't know!" Then I show my American driver's license, and they always let me go."

# Chapter 15
# Nocturnal Vatican

Whenever I go to the Vatican, my visit is colored by my own experience; my memories reach back to the papacy of John Paul II when communism in Eastern Europe started to crack, and I felt like I was at the center of cataclysmic changes. I remember walking through St. Peter's Square in 1984 one morning and saw posters plastered everywhere about the murder of Jerzy Popiełuszko, a Polish priest. He was an outspoken critic of the Russian backed regime. Europe was on the brink of change, the Pope was an important stakeholder, and I was there. When I returned years later, the Vatican held greater historical importance for me. As I wandered through Raphael's Rooms and looked up at the School of Athens, where all the ancient world's wisdom was summarized, I was surrounded by history. I realized that humanism, in which humanity was exalted to the center of the universe, was celebrated in this spot by Michelangelo, Raphael, and even the Renaissance Popes, despite their faults. Again, I felt I was at the center of cultural change.

On this visit, I wanted to experience the spiritual angle, so I got up early on the advice of a friend and entered St. Peter's Basilica at the moment it opened at 7 a.m. The church was silent, there was nobody there, but a dozen or so priests and laypeople, and the light shone through the upper windows with such delineated shafts that they appeared to be some type of transporter devices.

I stood in the back and looked up, nodding. Yes, this is how St. Peter's is supposed to be experienced.

My friend also advised me to head downstairs to a private chapel right above the tomb of St. Peter; this chapel is closed during the tourist day and only open for services. Surely there would be a service there this early, I thought. As a priest rushed in with his chalice and three or four older women scurried in back of him to grab a place inside, I was not disappointed. The chapel looked like it could only hold about fifteen people, so I grabbed my spot at the apostle's grave.

I could barely hear the priest and tried to mutter the Italian responses, but after a while, I grew silent and reflected on the privilege of being in that place. I thought of Peter, the man rather than Peter, the apostle, who could be impetuous and unthinking yet loving and loyal. The man who denied Christ yet loved him and could relate to someone like me who doesn't always live up to his beliefs. When he failed, his love outweighed his guilt, and he came back; I could relate to that. He wasn't a great scholar, he didn't leave a lot of writings, and he never sought to be the center of attention. But here he lay, not because of what he said, but because of his love. Here I am, near the tomb of this man whose life became defined not by trying to be perfect but by his love for his Christ.

After the service was over, I made my way up to the main basilica again to enjoy the last moments before the hoards appeared. I had so many memories here: of the priest in confession who told me I had to leave the seminary because I experienced sexual desires; of the high altar where I was a server and was able to meet the Pope; of a conversation I overheard as an Italian man pointed to the marble on the floor and told his American companion that the design resembled her vagina; of walking up the stairs when I was a seminarian and noticing that Mother Theresa was walking next to me with the rest of the crowd; of the quiet times I spent in one of the chapels when I lived within walking distance; of the midnight Masses on Christmas Eve always full of American military families; of Easter week, full of unending ceremonies and beautiful chanting; memories of the honor and privilege I felt to be standing in that spot where Christians scratched into a rock "Peter is here," where Constantine built his basilica and where Michelangelo, Bernini, and others erected a new one. I was here, on this spot where I have been so many times before. And yet, every time it was different.

By this time, tourists were pouring in. But I had another visit on my list: the Vatican Museums.

The walk from the basilica to the museums seemed endless as I dodged street vendors, gypsies, priests, nuns, and tourist groups. I was determined to get there before opening in order, hopefully, to avoid the line, but to no avail. I thought the opening was at 10 a.m., but instead, it was at 9, and it was now 9:30. The line stretched along the block and was growing; I jumped in to reserve my place and reflect if I should stay or return another day. The line was not moving, so I decided to ask the person in the back of me to hold my place while I walked up to the entrance to see the situation. The line was not moving as tickets were being processed; as I turned to go back, a poster caught my eye; "Vatican Museum on Friday Nights" it read. The poster described fewer crowds and more opportunities to enjoy the art; the museum would stay open until 11 p.m. That was enough for me; I took off and planned to return that evening.

It was 8 p.m. when I rearrived at the museum, and this time there was no line at all. I walked in, paid for my ticket, and I found myself immersed in the collection within five minutes.

I expected to encounter a barrage of counter-reformation art but instead found myself in ancient Egypt, standing amid the Egyptian collection. The rooms felt like an Egyptian tomb with some Roman decor, and the atmosphere was dark, eerie, and very cool. As I wandered through the nine rooms of the Gregorian Egyptian Museum, I soon found myself in the *Reconstruction of the Serapeum of the Canopus* of Hadrian's Villa, which was laid out as the statues could have been displayed at the time of Hadrian. These artifacts were discovered in the 1700s while looking for Antinous's tomb, who was Hadrian's lover. Antinous died in a tragic accident in the Nile at age 20; after this, not wanting to let go of his memory, Hadrian deified the youth; statues of Antinous, dressed in Egyptian garb, sprang up all over the empire.

The stories surrounding the death of Antinous vary from suicide, murder, to bleeding to death by castrating himself; none of these is based on fact, and the most likely scenario is accidental drowning. Based on Hadrian's reaction, the truth is that there was deep love between the two men. Not much is known about Antinous, and most of it is conjecture; he was probably of humble origins, had a basic education, and was from what is now Turkey. The facts about Antinous include the date of 125 CE when he became Hadrian's favorite. The emperor believed Antinous to be intelligent and wise. Both shared an interest in hunting, leading to the story of Hadrian saving Antinous from an attack of a mountain lion in Libya in 130 CE, a much-publicized event. The two became inseparable, traveling around the empire together; Hadrian seemed to crave Antinous's very presence, and there is no evidence that the latter ever used his position for personal gain. There is evidence that their relationship was sexual and that Hadrian preferred the presence of men and boys to women; the emperor's marriage was an unhappy one, his wife being Vibia Sabina, a political alliance. A homosexual relationship in the ancient world did not carry the "scandal" that it acquired in some sectors later in history. Hadrian and Antinous felt no compulsion to hide the nature of their relationship.

As I stood before this statue of Antinous I thought of how sad it was: the emperor was so heartbroken when he lost the one he loved that the only way to hold on to him was to make him a god, and have him worshipped throughout the empire. Did Hadrian believe Antinous was divine? Probably not, but knowing that his image would be honored throughout his realm would have brought some consolation to his lonely heart.

It was time to move forward and, rather than trying to see every single object in the museum this night, I would just stop and linger at pieces that spoke to me. In this spirit, I soon found myself in the Pio Clementino section, standing in front of the Laocoon. The twisting bodies, father and sons, wrapped by serpents poised to attack the man in the center. This nightmare scene stems from the Trojan War, in which a Trojan priest serving Apollo, whose name was Laocoon, was warning his fellow Trojans not to bring that wooden horse inside the city gates. As Laocoon stood there speaking, his small sons beside him, he didn't notice two serpents emerging from the sea behind him. The snakes wrapped themselves around the man and two boys and began dragging them out to sea, while Laocoon kept shouting his warnings to the Trojans. Dragged beneath the foamy waters to their deaths, Athena and Poseidon celebrated their triumph as Troy opened its gates, and the wooden horse was brought inside. I was looking at that moment when Laocoon, perceiving the future, struggled to thwart Troy's fate laid down by the gods, but he failed. His face was full of despair and futility, suffering from no hope for redemption or deliverance from his fate.

There were tragedy and beauty here, wrapped up into a scene of idealized bodies, contorted faces, and the serpents as the agents of death. The scene was essential to the Romans, who derived their place in history from Troy's royal house, from which Aeneas, founder of Rome, derived his ancestry. The Laocoon implies that Aeneas and his followers were following the will of the gods when they fled the cursed Troy and made their way to the area of Rome, becoming the progenitors of the Romans and a vast empire. By staking their origins both in Troy's royal house and the workings of the gods, the Romans could justify the expanding of their empire and the relegation of the known world to Roman rule.

The statue was found in 1506, and some sources claim it stood in Nero's Golden House, which wouldn't be surprising given his fascination with all things having to do with Troy. Here I stood, looking at this statue gazed upon by emperors, Popes, and Renaissance artists. For some, the figure spoke of a historical narrative; for others, it expressed the dawning of humanism, and for still others, it was the pinnacle of artistic expression. For me, however, standing there in that moment, the statue was sad and tragic; a man and his sons crying out in fear, unable to stop fate, about to face their end as they struggle to free themselves from the inevitable.

The hope only came afterward, when a man and a few followers escaped Troy and landed here, giving rise to this city where I now stood.

I wanted a break from sculpture, so I headed over to the Pinacoteca, the painting gallery, to see if something spoke to me. I went in and out of a few rooms, enjoying the mostly Christian art, until I found myself in the sixteenth-century collection, standing in front of Raphael's *Transfiguration*.

I'm not a great fan of paintings in which Christ's face is feminized, and the rosy cheeks in this painting put me off at first, but I decided to stay and look at the scene as a whole since there was something here beckoning me.

Traditionally this painting is analyzed in two parts, but I see three: Christ transfigured, three disciples, shielding their eyes, and the tumult below surrounding a sick child. Since the painting draws my eyes up, I looked at that Christ floating in the air on Mount Tabor, surrounded by Moses, representing the law, and Elias, representing the prophets. There are two smaller men on the side, representing the saints who were the patrons of the church for which this painting was commissioned, so I ignored them. But looking up to that top half of the picture, I see relationships: Moses and Elias, with all they represent, look at the Christ, who doesn't look back at them but gazes up towards someone else. Relationships: Old and New Testaments, a way of living guided by rules and texts and another way only hinted at. The Christ in this painting doesn't hold a tablet, like Moses, or a book, like Elias; the only thing he has is a calm and precise gaze towards another.

In the middle section are three men who are, according to the story in the Gospel of Matthew, Peter, James, and John; on seeing this Christ they knew so well now transfigured into something they didn't understand, they were stunned. Then the impetuous Peter offered to build some tents for the three, so they could stay on Tabor and make this all a permanent arrangement. They then heard a voice declaring him to be "...my son, whom I love and in whom I am pleased..." (Matthew 17: 1-8). This is where the second scene in the painting comes into play because hearing the voice and seeing the transfiguration, the three men appear to cover their eyes, and one is even hiding. Their reaction seems to stem from the realization that they are in the presence of something so much greater than themselves that they are struck silent, their eyes unable to gaze, and their minds unable to analyze. They realize that they are in the presence of mystery. Maybe Einstein expressed it best:

*The most beautiful thing we can experience is the mysterious. It is the source of all true art and science. He to whom the emotion is a stranger, who can no longer pause to wonder and stand wrapped in awe, is as good as dead —his eyes are closed.*

(Albert Einstein, Living Philosophies).

When I look to the bottom part of the painting, which is darker, there is disagreement, confusion, problems to be dealt with, points of view to be compared, suffering, illness, curiosity, and just about every human emotion experienced. I realized that this is my world. I could relate to this part of the painting most easily.

Raphael guides our eyes to look at the sick or possessed child as the third scene's focus, but the confusion around the child bewilders the eye. Some are looking on in curiosity, indifferent to the child. Others are entirely distracted, involved in their affairs and conversations. Others seem to want to help the child but don't know how to. Suggestions are being made; analysis is being put forth. It's almost as if the townspeople are pushing this child towards the apostles and are saying: "Do something!" but there is no agreement about what to do. There is also one arm from a man on the left hand of the painting, and a hand from a man on the right, pointing to the scene above. How are these different scenes connected? What do the challenges and needs of daily life have to do with faith? More than that, what is the nexus between human need and divine presence? Raphael doesn't answer this question but hints at it in this painting.

I walked away from that room, reflecting on the whole Renaissance thrust in the direction of humanism. For centuries, faith experience was divorced from the world; much of medieval art depicts saints or figures far away from the life that regular humans have to live. Medieval saints live in backgrounds of gold and sit on thrones. But with the Renaissance, people began to wonder whether being human was all that bad.

Humanism in Italy met fertile ground because its culture didn't favor an absolute divide between God and man. As classical works were rediscovered in monastic libraries or brought to light by crusaders in the East, it was churchmen such as Petrarch, Cardinal Basilios Bessarion, Pope Pius II, Sixtus IV, and Leo X, who had the insight to be open to and embrace classical knowledge and culture. It was like a lost treasure that had been overlooked and obscured during the Middle Ages when the art of surviving was more pressing than becoming a well-rounded, educated individual. But when prosperity grew, cities could become centers of culture and learning, and the knowledge of the past could help illuminate life in the present.

When his friends lowered Renaissance artist Pinturicchio through a hole deep into the earth near the coliseum, and as Pinturicchio held his candle up to view the structure and artwork that nobody had seen in a thousand years in the buried Golden House of Nero, he could not have imagined the revolution that this and other discoveries would ignite. No longer would the world be separated into "pagan" and "Christian" since all beauty and knowledge could be experienced as reflections of the greatness of man and his Creator. After climbing out of that hole on that afternoon in about 1480, the artist could never have foreseen that the sense of awe that he brought to the surface would permeate and transform the medieval view of the world, which became more human and yet even more divine. Man was no longer divorced from God.

I found the Vatican museums fascinating because they were created on the premise that human expression, whether religious or not, are all facets of the same unique truth: that the human being is the most amazing and clear image of the divine. Unabashedly "secular," unashamedly "religious"; Renaissance humanism simply didn't recognize this divide and what I saw this evening demonstrated this.

# Conclusions

A journey through Rome begins with the visitor as the stories between the past and present converge together. We find ourselves immeshed in the legends surrounding churches and monuments, fountains, and neighborhoods, experiencing good and evil, saints and weirdos in the past and present. Humanity flocks to this city, which overflows with examples of heroism and corruption on the same street! Since ancient Rome, the city's life has been on its streets, with its performers, cafes and crowds from practically every country and culture. The contemporary street artists, surrounded by spectators in jeans and tennis shoes, echo those in the ancient world, in sandals and togas. In Rome, history comes alive because it invades all five senses. The visitor can see the soaring ceilings of Caracalla's ancient baths and touch that wall where Nero perhaps leaned and hear the gurgling of the underground stream at the Mamertine Prison; the daring can even taste the ancient world!

The charm of Rome is the ability to get lost on purpose and discover something new and precious or unique, like a little-visited piazza, a neighborhood that still bears the scars of the last world war or a fountain that is a monument to love. The city is often filled with American tourists whose amazement is contagious and expectations that everything functions as it does in their country are comical. Each American and tourist from other countries have their favorite places to eat, where even the restaurants in this magical place have their stories. Whether it is a cafe connected to a Pontifical university, a comfortable bar with a generous happy hour, or a luxury dining experience run by an order of nuns, the stories leap from the menus. It is the people who give meaning to the statues, monuments, food, and art that fills Rome, and the Romans themselves, who have lived there for one generation or more, each have their unique experience of what the city means.

Most visitors miss the fascinating part of the city, which is underground Rome. The Golden House of Nero, the homes of Augustus and Livia, the catacombs and other excavated areas are like time capsules which transport one back to where the walls speak and the frescoes cry out, expressing even after death the desires, beliefs, and values of those who lived or were buried there. Italians who immigrated to Rome often have a different perspective. Their bond to the history of the city is powerful; they explore Rome above and underground and are often the first to discover the most unique and unknown aspects of the city.

No artist captures Rome's spirit better than Caravaggio, whose grittiness, realism, sensuality, lack of discipline, spirituality, and connection to the divine somehow result in masterpieces that those who followed him could only try to imitate. Following his footsteps in Rome and absorbing the expressiveness of his art, the visitor gains a glimpse into Rome's essence, which is somewhere between the human and the divine. And yet, following the artist's path in the city today, one notices the people watching, eating, selling, performing, and wandering. Each person has their story, their background, their hopes, and dreams. A judgmental attitude, regulating people into stereotypes, is difficult to maintain in Rome because the city's international character keeps revealing that humans are not who they may seem to be at first.

Those who want to drink deeper of Rome's magical potion venture into the lesser-visited areas, whether outside the city to surrounding towns or a lesser-known museum within the historical center. Taking some risk in going outside the beaten tourist path always rewards in this place where one can find oneself as the lone visitor or explorer in an area that few tourists venture.

But who has the inside scoop on what Rome is? The expats give the perspective of an outsider, with often comical stories of dealing with Roman bureaucracy; the Romans are aware of the city's potential, which is often not realized, and the Italians who have immigrated there tend to ignore the shortcomings and enjoy the grandeur of Rome. The expats, however, have the funniest stories.

This visit to Rome concludes with a nocturnal Vatican visit. Wandering through the darkened halls, surrounded by art from Egypt, Nero's Golden House, Caracalla's baths, and the ancient Greek world, the realization growing that Rome hangs somehow between the human and divine, just as expressed in Caravaggio's work.

Rome's history is never concluded because the stories continue in the personal lives of those who bond with the city. This book is an invitation to experience Rome in its stories, which give meaning to a monument, a painting, the street performer, the expat, the restaurant owner, and the ghosts of those long dead. Those who experience Rome's magic understand that beyond the dirty streets, the graffiti, and all the problems with mismanagement that one can spend time complaining about, there is something else that cannot be found elsewhere. Those visitors who allow themselves to experience this "something else" will carry memories of their visit away and carry its magic with them. The city will eventually beckon them back because she is a jealous lover and does not want to be forgotten by those she has seduced.

Rome teaches that it is the story that matters and that beyond the tasks and responsibilities of life, there is a greater context that gives meaning to the fabric of human existence. One realizes that it is not the "thing" that matters as much as the story behind it. Rome is this collection of stories embedded in the buildings, ruins, people, and hidden angles. For this reason, the city is eternal because the stories continue.

# Acknowledgments

Taking time out of their busy day to share their story is not an easy task for those I interviewed, so I want to express my gratitude to Francesco Ciccone, owner/manager of *Sphaeristerium Ristobar*[22] and to his team Fabiano and Cristina; to the street performers Federica Tranchida (The Sparkle)[23] and Ann Louise Amendolagine[24], To Jonathan, who has been a fixture and catalyst for change in Rome for all of his 80 plus years.

I would also like to thank the expats who agreed to be interviewed, such as Maazouza, Rachel, and Kevin. I also thank the Romans Lilli, Sergio, Lorenza, and Carmela together with Franco and Massimo and all non-Roman Italians living in the city, along with all those whose faces make the fabric of these stories.

---

22 https://www.sphaeristerium.it
23 https://www.thesparklefire.com
24 www.facebook.com/ann.amendolagine